THE AGE OF SAIL IN
THE AGE OF AQUARIUS

THE AGE OF SAIL IN THE AGE OF AQUARIUS

The South Street Seaport and the Crisis of the Sixties

ROBIN K. FOSTER

ISBN: 1523953276
ISBN 13: 9781523953271
Library of Congress Control Number: 2016902623
CreateSpace Independent Publishing Platform
North Charleston, South Carolina

For Clem

And for my boys: *Find what brings you joy, and go there*

Many thanks to the good and gracious people who have helped me along the way. To my teachers and advisors: Ricki Lombardo at D-S Regional High School, whose Theater of the Absurd class lives on, so many years later, in stories from all who rose to that wonderful challenge; to Clark Brown at NYU, who recognized early on that "Robin doesn't do bullsh#t;" to the incomparable Stanley Katz at Princeton; to Jim Goodman at Rutgers, who stepped in at a critical juncture; to my dearly missed friend Clement Price at Rutgers, who was my friend/mentor/champion/teacher-in-all-things, all rolled up inside one remarkable and truly gracious human being.

Thank you to the Rockefeller Archive Center, the New-York Historical Society, and the South Street Seaport Museum for assistance with their valuable collections.

Thank you to my family, especially my mom and dad.

Deep and special thanks to Stan, who gets me.

TABLE OF CONTENTS

Introduction · xi

Chapter 1 Postwar Pastoral; Miller, Mumford and
Rethinking Modernism · 1
Chapter 2 Battle Lines Being Drawn ·33
Chapter 3 Past Perfect; History and Identity on the Waterfront · · · · · · · 66
Chapter 4 Battle of the Port; Preservation and Commemoration
at the South Street Seaport ·101

Conclusion ·135
Author's Note ·142
Notes· ·144
Bibliography ·177

INTRODUCTION

*The city does not tell its past, but contains it like the lines
of a hand, written in the corners of the streets, the gratings
of the windows, the banisters of the steps, every segment
marked in turn with scratches, indentations, scrolls.*[1]

- Italo Calvino, Invisible Cities (1972)

In the spring of 1967, amidst the backdrop of social, political, and cultural fracturing that characterized those long hot summers between 1966 and 1968, a grassroots preservation start-up known as the Friends of South Street procured a charter from the State of New York Board of Regents for the creation of the South Street Seaport Museum. Situated along the East River in lower Manhattan, South Street Seaport was conceived "to tell the story of the men in ships who built the city's greatness in the century that the young American republic came of age."[2] Fundamental to the founding vision behind the Seaport Museum were two questions: *what has our city become?* And *what do we want this city to be?* Preservation and commemoration of the city's oldest maritime district was "intended to weave back into the fabric of city life some of the warmth and accessibility that have been lost along the way," and to provide a vital amenity to the shape that the modern city had become.[3] Early writings from Museum founders and supporters indicate a concern not only with the question, *what has our city become?* But query more broadly: *who are we?* And *what have **we** become?*

Echoing *antimodern* sentiments found in the writings of Nathaniel Hawthorne, Frederick Law Olmsted, and Henry Miller, Museum founder Peter Stanford's plans for the South Street Seaport Museum were steeped in a pastoral yearning for a more heroic era, one which might guide the city forward. Could Stanford's plans to bring *windships* to the city's old seaport actually teach New Yorkers about a slower pace of life amidst the hurried cacophony of the modern urban environment?[4] The sailing ship represented a remedy to the modern paradox of the machine in the garden. Not a noisy locomotive barreling through the pastoral landscape, offending the senses of smell, sight, and sound; the sailing ship – whether schooner, square-rigger, or lightship - instead represented a pastoral idyll in the chaos of the machine that was postwar era New York City. The sailing ship conjured imagery of a nineteenth century way of life, in which man was more directly tied to the elements and to nature, in which one worked with his hands, practiced his craft, and was not simply a cog in the industrial machine.[5]

When he christened his own schooner *Athena,* Stanford recalled the days of the ancient Greek agora, when the city served as a meeting place where citizens gathered to talk about philosophy, government, and the deepest meanings of the human condition. The ideals and functions of the original democratic city-state inspired Stanford during his own socio-political climate, where "in a time of unrest in city streets and college campuses, we admired the classic moderation of the Greek civilization, which shone for us like a beacon." The cultural dissent and disruption manifesting in anti-war protests, campus takeovers, and the urban riots of the late 1960s were not relegated to the sidelines of the Friends' vision for a restored South Street Seaport but in fact informed its very foundation. Indicating a critical sensibility was lacking in the present cultural landscape, Jakob Istanbrandt, shipping magnate and original chairman of the South Street Seaport Museum, emphasized these plans at South Street were about more than restoring windships from the past; this was about *a return to fundamentals.*[6]

Just as Herman Melville and Ernest Hemingway had done through literature, with *Moby Dick, Billy Budd,* and *Old Man and the Sea,* Stanford and the Friends of South Street sought to bring the romance and heroism of the sea to life. For it was at sea, Stanford felt, where one faced the "honest realities" of life, and if one was going to make it at all, one had to make it by his wits and his God-given gifts. A local sea captain insisted, "Schooners like this were sailed by a different breed of men." Ours is, historically, a maritime nation, and the seafaring life is the heritage of all Americans. To the Friends of South Street, South Street's history was an important collective history, one that recalled a tough life, a hard life, but one that "was clean and free and held satisfaction."[7] *Clean and free and held satisfaction.* Dignity. Tough, but free.

This is the stuff of traditional American hero myths, and we see these hero myths play out in maritime-inspired characters from Melville's Captain Ahab to Conrad's Billy Budd to *On the Waterfront's* Terry Malloy to Hemingway's Old Man Santiago: *a different breed of men,* each inextricably tied to the sea. Their relationship to the sea made each of these men better. Stronger. More dignified. The South Street Seaport Museum extended this heritage of dignity and strength to the cobbled streets and old brick walls of Fulton Street and Schermerhorn Row, where Stanford and Friends hoped to rekindle some of South Street's former glory during its heyday in the mid-nineteenth century, a time when the East River seaport had been the economic hub for the entire city.[8]

Fundamentally at stake in the preservation of the old cityscape was *meaning,* during a time characterized by lack of consensus on any meaning, whether cultural, political, or racial; a time when the country was divided between hawk and dove, right and left, straight and freak, black and white. With the nation's escalation into the Vietnam War raising questions both political and moral, Stanford and South Street's early supporters were intent on creating something valuable for the city, while each in his own way continued to protest the divisive foreign war. On the home front, Stanford found the counterculture revolution disheartening, and lamented the veneration of "meaninglessness" that had become part of the modern grievance. Stanford felt he was speaking for his entire generation; the project at South Street was meant to resuscitate the value inherent in old brick and cobbled streets of the seaport district, storehouses of memory that could teach something much needed in the meaningless present and into the uncertain future. Looking back on the '60s from several decades hence, Stanford recalls in his memoir, "The people of our generation clearly, and very nearly unanimously, felt the same."[9]

We must understand, then, that while conventional wisdom explains the resurgence of historic preservation in New York City following the 1963 destruction of Pennsylvania Station as a reaction against the physical transformations of the urban landscape in the name of urban renewal, preservation and commemoration of the cultural and physical landscape was more deeply rooted in notions of collective identity and cultural meaning. The Federalist era buildings lining Schermerhorn Row *meant* something to the Friends of the Seaport, just as the unfurled masts of a schooner sailing into South Street *meant* something. These reminders of the maritime past evoked a panorama of values found wanting in the present cultural landscape of the late 1960s.

BORN IN AN IDENTITY CRISIS

We read cultural productions - artistic and literary representations - of the waterfront in order to understand the ways in which these aesthetic depictions of the landscape helped to create a very particular urban identity. Why do we care about streetscapes, architecture, and things in the first place, and why it is that seemingly disparate actors and communities attached particular significance to the myth of a more heroic collective identity in the midst of a current cultural crisis? Conventional wisdom surrounding the re-emergence of historic preservation in the 1960s places extraordinary focus on a collective distress with modernism's zeal for urban renewal and the subsequent physical transformation of the city under an increasingly centralized planning authority.

The historic preservation boom of the 1960s was born in an identity crisis, in which insecurities and anxieties festered amidst a rapidly changing and turbulent world. The preservation impulse in the 1960s arose as part of a larger conversation on American identity during a time of vocal challenge and dissent to the status quo, a full decade before historic preservation as an urban revitalization strategy emerged in the late 1970s and flourished with the ubiquitous festival marketplace in the 1980s and '90s. Collective memory, informed by the narrative of historic preservation, is a tool used to legitimate group identity amidst an uncertain and hyper-changing world. We must understand how and by whom memories are shaped for collective consumption; what do public memories attempt to legitimate during periods of challenge and dissent? The nostalgic impulse fueled simultaneous maritime-inspired preservation projects in lower Manhattan in the late-1960s, when growing anxieties created by the restructuring of American society manifested in a sentimental yearning for a collective memory that was itself a myth; an idealized conception of the past born from present-day anxieties about the changing political, economic, and social landscape.

The 1960s' resurgence of historic preservation involved a process of shoring up cultural authority and recalling a more heroic personal and collective narrative amidst the political and cultural turmoil of that decade. While support for historic preservation of the mid-nineteenth century cityscape was gaining momentum in lower Manhattan, cities were besieged by social and political upheaval and dissent. Urban historian Jon Teaford remarks upon this age of urban crisis, in which, "as was so often the case in the late 1960s and 1970s, the most dire news was from New York City."[10] It is important to note that this process of shoring up cultural authority, the cultural authority of an era which produced "a different breed of men," is nuanced; is informed through an appreciation for official as well as vernacular history; and does not necessarily constitute a partisan conservative consensus. The motivating sensibilities behind this process are as diverse as the actors involved. Stanford and the Friends of South Street focused on the restoration of sailing ships and teaching the craftsmanship and vernacular history of maritime trade, recalling an era when life's rhythms were at once slower and also attuned to the "daring, sacrifice, and endurance"[11] which emerged from a life battling the sea. At the same time, counterculture supporters like musician Pete Seeger promoted a radical left-leaning political sensibility, while the lower

Manhattan business community, led by David Rockefeller, sought to realize its own historic preservation project recalling traditional patriotism and heroism of the Revolutionary War era. Diverse actors on the growing historic preservation scene in the late 1960s in lower Manhattan chased diverse notions of exactly *whose* cultural authority demanded revitalization. The consensus lies in the *process* of revitalizing a more desirable identity or collective meaning during an era of cultural dislocation.

The historic preservation movement of the 1960s, illustrated here through the development of the South Street Seaport Museum and the Fraunces Tavern museum block project, emerged during that decade's sense of unraveling of the American cultural landscape, and was part of a larger cultural dynamic of the period which alternately questioned, challenged, and supported the status quo. More specifically, preservation and commemoration of the nation's maritime roots during the cultural and political ferment of the late 1960s sought to revitalize the personal and collective identity of an era that had produced *a different breed of men*, an era which appeared to folks on many sides of the political and socio-economic spectrum to embody a more noble sense of roots and pride, a sense presently wanting in the cultural landscape.

The return to historic preservation as an urban necessity is not simply the story of a dawning new urbanism, but indicates a more complicated shift, one that places the historic preservation movement within a larger cultural crisis that openly questioned the tenuous notion of an American identity. Both the South Street Seaport Museum - supported by New York State Senator Whitney Seymour, Peter Stanford, Friends of South Street, shipping magnate Jakob Istanbrandt, and numerous maritime aficionados; and the Fraunces Tavern museum block project - garnering even wider support from the Sons of the Revolution, the downtown financial community led by David Rockefeller and Chase Manhattan Bank, the Museum of the City of New York, and several key offices in City administration - envisioned commemoration of the Golden Age of Sail as streetscape preservation on a neighborhood scale. Ranging from historic preservation to history-inspired re-creation, the objectives of both the South Street Seaport and the Fraunces Tavern projects meant to recreate a streetscape evocative of the city's roots in maritime trade and create collective memories of a time *when we were good.*

Existing scholarship has tended to locate the rise of historic preservation in the 1960s as a response to the destructive course of the urban renewal bulldozer and the aesthetic void of modern urban planning. Conventional wisdom cites Jane Jacobs' *The Death and Life of Great American Cities* as the seminal rallying cry against federally funded urban renewal and the ongoing razing of *blighted* downtown districts. Postwar urban renewal incited visceral opposition from architecture journalist Jacobs and sociologist Herbart Gans, who travelled up and down the Eastern seaboard, writing extensively on the sociological impact of postwar urban restructuring on local communities.[12] At stake was the city's cultural and historic landscape, its very livability.

Jane Jacobs' *The Death and Life of Great American Cities* is still perhaps the most highly influential text on the development of contemporary urban planning and the need for preservation of the old cityscape. Jacobs' community-based vision for urban growth and sustainability served as a catalyst for civil rights era community activism in neighborhood planning through her rejection of modernism's ruthless savagery and centralized approach to local urban concerns. Challenging the architect and urban planner Le Corbusier's modernist rant, "Death of the street!" Jacobs insisted mixed-use streets and busy sidewalks were critical elements of any vital city. More recently, contemporary critics have challenged Jacobs' vision, asserting her woman-on-the-street vantage point ignored the contentious issues of racial segregation that had been festering for decades, a vantage point that directly contributed to an ever-growing tide of NIMBY'ism. Still, Jacobs' vision for a more locally-controlled urbanism reflects a larger ideological shift, where by the 1970s, a growing disillusionment with liberalism and New Deal/Great Society policies signaled "the fate of liberalism hung in the balance in a postwar struggle over rights, racial identity and taxation."[13] Inspired by Jacobs' impassioned and vernacular tone, a growing cadre of historic preservationists, upper-class urban dwellers, and grassroots community preservationists rallied against the physical reconfiguration of cities at the hands of a tightly centralized authority during this *age of urban crisis.*

Urban historian Jon Teaford coined this term – *the age of urban crisis* – to describe the myriad urban woes infecting Eastern and Midwestern cities during the post-World War II era. During the Cold War era, Jacobs, Gans, urban critic Lewis Mumford, editors from *TIME* and *LIFE* magazines, keynote speakers at both Democratic and Republican conventions, and emerging scions of rock'n'roll remarked with increasing urgency on a proliferating unrest and disease affecting the nation's urban centers. Contemporary historians and cultural critics examine the ruins left in the wake of a national trend towards decentralization and deindustrialization, increasing violence associated with the struggle for racial equality and civil rights, and the age of fracture in the postwar metropolis.

By the 1960s, a search for *authenticity* and a growing interest in the commodification of history evolved as a means to address the postwar urban crisis. Brooklyn's history-inspired *brownstoning* movement dates to the 1940s, when artists and white-collar professionals sought out the borough's cheaper housing prices as the Manhattan real estate market soared. By the 1960s, these gentrifiers – predominantly white (99%), educated (99.9%), and affluent (98.3%) - promoted a return to an earlier iteration of urban living, idealizing close-knit housing and vibrant street life in the midst of monotony, conformity, and an increasingly bureaucratic city.[14] Brooklyn brownstoners latched on to the historic value of these neighborhoods – and invented charming names such as Boerum Hill, Carrol Gardens, and Prospect Heights – in response to the urban renewal bulldozer and the effect it had on both real estate values *and* the city's walkability and intimacy. "Authentic" neighborhoods could still be found across the East River. For these brownstoners, nostalgia and romanticism mingled with a political sensibility that challenged centralized government, urban renewal policies, and failed postwar liberal programs.[15] Historic preservation in the postwar decades grew, in part, out of this response to federally-funded urban renewal, spurring grassroots efforts and the creation of local community development corporations.[16]

This search for *authenticity* occurs during moments of instability and crisis, when identities are unstable. By the 1960s, American cities were increasingly described as malignant, and hopeless victims of a widespread urban crisis. At the same time, diverse community and preservation groups responded to postwar urban renewal policies that funded the razing of poor and working class neighborhoods in favor of massive public housing projects and government centers. These historic preservationists, community activists, and gentrifiers "spoke up for authenticity," for a different kind of city, in which *all* residents, not simply the wealthy, corporate, and government interests, retained their rights to the city.[17] While urban scholars have primarily attributed the rise of 1960s' historic preservation as a reaction against federal urban renewal policy, private redevelopment, and the local political alliances that made widespread razing of the urban landscape possible, we must consider a broader cultural landscape – and deeper questions surrounding collective identity and cultural meaning- from which the preservation movement emerged.

While the deindustrialization and decentralization of cities had begun its long march south, west, and all points suburban in the 1920s, the full impact of the urban crisis became readily apparent following World War II's brief economic boom. In the 1950s and '60s, urban crime rates soared; Eastern and Midwestern cities continued to suffer decentralization and an ongoing exodus to the suburbs and Sunbelt; racial tensions fueled violent civil protests across the nation. Teaford has noted, "The disintegration of the city was readily apparent."[18] In September 1967, *U.S. News and World Report* asked, "Can the Big Cities Ever Come Back?" Citing riots, skyrocketing crime, and ongoing financial problems, the report concluded, "The crisis of the big cities, coming to a head in recent years, continues without let up."[19]

Modern urban planning's solution to the social and economic ills of the city was found in the physical restructuring of its hodgepodge and antiquated urban core. Build it better, newer, glossier, and businesses and middle-class consumers will come. One might understand the impetus - however sociologically misguided - to raze block after block of dilapidated tenement housing leftover from the nineteenth century in order to build, for example, the United Nations Building along Manhattan's East River waterfront. One could not fathom, however, the demolition of that majestically-inspired and glorious architectural achievement of Pennsylvania Station, only fifty-four years old and yet, in the days of decreasing rail travel, already an untenable financial hardship on its owners, the Pennsylvania Railroad Company.

Conventional wisdom locates the formation of New York City's postwar historic preservation movement in that 1964 destruction of Penn Station. However, historians Max Page and Randall Mason place the 1960s' historic preservation impulse within a larger historical trajectory, rooted in Progressive Era social reform. Historic preservation was, therefore, not new to the 1960s, and yet the cultural landscape of the postwar era – including the physical demolition of architecture both grand and vernacular, *and* the age of urban crisis – informed its resurgence.

Of course, when we think of downtown historic preservation in the con-temporary cityscape, we usually think in terms of economic revitalization plans so prevalent in recent decades. The redevelopment of Boston's Faneuil Hall, Baltimore's Inner Harbor, and New York's SoHo speak to the commercial re-vitalization motivation behind downtown historic preservation. In fact, festival marketplaces had become the "hottest fad" of 1980s commercial development and by the 1990s, historic preservation had become *the most popular strategy* for revitalizing smaller downtown American cities because visitors respond to envi-ronments laced with nostalgia.[20] We tend to find these neighborhoods *charming*. And while San Francisco's Ghirardelli Square waterfront redevelopment proves a strong example of early commercial revitalization via historic rehabilitation, in the early 1960s this project was more than a decade ahead of the national trend.

Looking to the past in order to build a new city had started to become an economic and commercial revitalization strategy only by the late 1970s, after the National Trust for Historic Preservation had launched its Main Street Pilot Program. Using the principles of historic preservation, the downtown redevelopment of small cities like Hot Springs, South Dakota; Madison, Indiana; and Galesburg, Illinois yielded uneven successes but sparked a na-tional trend towards the marketing of nostalgia in order to revitalize flagging downtown districts. With *the past* now understood by urban planners as a marketable commodity, historic preservation became a national strategy in commercial revitalization, fueled by a nostalgia for classic architectural styles and the patrimony of the generations from which those styles emerged.

Architectural historian M. Christine Boyer's skepticism of festival market-places and the manufactured charm-factor of cobbled downtown cityscapes uncovers the "stench of nostalgia" used to pervert the public's sense of history. There is no wharf rat, contagion, slave auction, or infant mortality in the consumable past. This argument has been well made in the collective litera-ture on memory, historic preservation, and the inevitable state of *nostalgia de la boue*: memory with the rough stuff taken out. The festival marketplace of the 1980s, the development of urban hipster neighborhoods like Georgetown, SoHo, and central Austin represent *exaggerated* visions of the myth of historic cityscapes and the lives they produced. What is critical to note here is Boyer's charge that this recollection of history *occurs most often in moments of crisis.* The current cultural landscape - whether this includes the physical razing of downtown city centers, social upheavals associated with racial strife, economic malaise of postindustrial decentralization, or vocal challenges to the nation's fundamental ideologies – informs the form and function of historic preserva-tion. Boyer notes the undercurrent of political agenda-making in the public sanction of historic preservation landscapes:

> Since a return to history most often occurs in moments of crisis, it is not surprising to find that city tableaux repeat visual ideals and normative views sanctioned by public authorities, who attempt in this manner *to regain a centered world or a concrete system on which moral, political, or social foundations can stand.*[21]

Our affection for history, then, rises and falls with the changing social-political-economic climate. During times of social crisis, concerted efforts to recall and rep-resent *the past* serve to shore up those very moral, political, and social foundations under threat. The razing of Penn Station was a siren call, to be sure, among New York City's historically and civically inclined populace. However, there is a more complicated cultural landscape marking the decade of the 1960s when downtown historic preservation felt its postwar resurgence. That complicated and often con-tentious cultural landscape provides a trove of evidence as to the necessity for re-membrance of a more heroic past during a decade of seemingly ubiquitous dissent.

The term *cultural landscape* denotes both the totality of all visible and material things that humans have added to, or subtracted from, the natural landscape of the earth *and* the matrix of cultural productions that mark a society's humanity, such as the arts, architecture, and language. The cultural landscape of lower Manhattan's waterfront district in the 1950s and '60s included the dilapidated piers and still-active shipping industry along the riverfront, the Mafia's continued control over the Port of New York, the seafood eateries sprinkled along Fulton and Water Streets, and the modernist office towers quickly replacing any remaining vestiges of the nineteenth century cityscape. The cultural landscape of New York City also included newsstands containing weekly issues of *TIME* and *LIFE* magazines reporting on the crisis of the week, living room television sets tuned to the *CBS Evening News with Walter Cronkite,* the student takeover of Columbia University, anti-war protests in Central Park, draft card burnings in front of the Whitehall Street induction center, and growing numbers of teenage hippies making their homes in Tompkins Square Park. Further, the cultural landscape is not static or uniform. Middle-class New Yorkers, their issues of *LIFE* magazine stacked on the coffee table and the television set to Walter Cronkite's nightly reporting, did not necessarily intersect with the marginalized cultural landscape of the waterfront Mafia scene or the Tompkins Square Park hippie scene, but likely gleaned this landscape through *LIFE* magazine's photo-essays or Hollywood's production of *On the Waterfront*.

Critical to note is not only the landscape itself, but more importantly *what we make of it*, what it means to various communities who travel within the cultural landscape. "Any landscape is composed not only of what lies before our eyes, but what lies within our heads."[22] That is, we read the cultural landscape not only for what it provides visually for our examination and interpretation, but for what it clarifies in our own minds. What did the cultural landscape of New York's South Street Seaport district mean to supporters of that maritime preservation project? What did the cultural landscape of the 1960s' seaport district represent, and what did its more glorious nineteenth century cultural landscape evoke and evince, in light of the social reality of the Sixties?

Looking back on the Sixties from three decades hence, political activist, writer and filmmaker Susan Sontag described the decade as "a sea-change in the whole culture, a trans-valuation of values – for which there are many names. Barbarism is one name for what was taking over. Let's use Nietzsche's term: we had entered, really entered, the age of nihilism."[23] Historians Maurice Isserman and Michael Kazin argue the Sixties was a time of intense conflict and change. Acknowledging no single narrative of the decade could possibly satisfy everybody, and cautiously arguing *the meaning* of the decade depends upon an individual's particular needs and/or observations, Isserman and Kazin nevertheless characterize the 1960s as a time when Americans suffered "an anguished scrutiny" over the nation's most fundamental institutions and value systems.[24]

Historian David Farber likewise engages in this sort of deep excavation towards uncovering what, fundamentally, explains the decades' sense of fracturing. Farber argues the decade experienced broad challenges to American common sense, because any previously held notions of common sense "had been subverted and hollowed out by the radical, political, cultural, and economic changes of the postwar era."[25] From civil rights demonstrators who practiced nonviolent resistance as a means "to turn the world upside down, invert the social order;" to the counterculture, which had become a mass-media phenomenon; to the dispatches from Vietnam via nightly news reports, which "magnified the confusing features of a war that, at best, was hard to fathom," contemporary historians recognize a ubiquitous challenge to America's political, racial, and social structures which converged in an existential crisis of national identity and legitimacy.[26] The cultural disruption and widespread turbulence of the decade, far from mere trope, has been recounted in reports and narratives from the moment they occurred *and* from contemporary historians who continue to examine the decade as a monumental time when many Americans openly questioned the very legitimacy of the nation's power structure because the state had "*failed to embody the ideals* and historical images American state makers had used to justify its very existence."[27] The 1960s and the 1930s are the only decades in modern times in which Americans across the spectrum actively questioned the nation's very survival.[28]

While the decade of the Sixties has been described in all manner of Technicolor and hyperbole in the four decades since, some recent conversations on the decade have questioned whether the Sixties were really as *far out* as we have been led to believe. Were the Sixties really so riotous? Were the Fifties, for that matter, really so conformist? If we are going to examine the role of historic preservation and the recollection of a heroic narrative in light of the existing cultural landscape, it behooves us to read the Sixties as the decade was written, by journalists and artists and writers and musicians who experienced their world in their own time.[29]

> *Greensboro 4..... Freedom Rides.... Southern Christian Leadership Conference.... Students for a Democratic Society... Student Nonviolent Coordinating Committee.....Congress Of Racial Equality....President John F. Kennedy assassinated...Malcolm X assassinated......Tet Offensive...Stop the Draft Week.... President LBJ won't seek another term.....Martin Luther King Jr. assassinated.... Black Power..... Columbia University occupation...Grand Central Station rally and police riot....Robert Kennedy assassinated....Democratic National Convention protest and police riot.....Riots in Philadelphia.....Watts..... Boston...Kansas City... Newark... Plainfield.....Detroit....Chicago.... Washington D.C... Baltimore...Stonewall....March on the Pentagon.... Black Panthers..... Woodstock.....Charles Manson.....My Lai.... Hey, hey LBJ, how many kids did you kill today?*

By 1968, cultural and political instability had fractured any remaining notions of American exceptionalism and split society along lines of race, class and generation. Mel Brooks said, "The world is being turned upside down, conventional wisdom is being thrown out the window." The counterculture, guided by the words of Abbie Hoffman and Jerry Rubin and Ken Kesey, scored by the music of Jimi Hendrix and Janis Joplin and Bob Dylan, fueled by marijuana and LSD, warned *Don't Trust Anyone Over 30*. The generation over 30 worried, too, informed by Pulitzer Prize -winning journalists writing for the *New York Times* on a hated war in a foreign land not understood.

Indeed, the fear of a violent present and uncertain future created an environ-ment in which feelings of nostalgia and the desire to preserve and/or re-create memories of a glorified past were intensified.

The 1960s represented a crisis of cultural authority, in all its possible rep-resentations and permutations. This crisis marked the decade during its own time and from a wide array of communities and populations, both domestic and abroad. The world witnessed global outrage and opposition in cities as di-verse as Prague, Paris, Moscow, and Mexico City. For a number of intrinsically complicated and nuanced reasons - far beyond our present scope - dissent and challenge, emanating primarily from a burgeoning youth population, character-ized the age. In America, the challenge against both domestic and foreign policy underscored an attack on the core of the nation's fundamental ideals and official dogma. At the core of this crisis of cultural authority was modernity itself:

> Under the impact of modernity, the beliefs, ideals, and traditions that [had] been central to Americans and to the character of American de-mocracy...[were] losing their cultural compelling power...Even those who say they believe in America's beliefs, traditions, and ideals no longer show that they do in ways that they once did or in ways that former generations did.[30]

> — Os Guinness.

The 1960s' crisis of cultural authority was certainly not the first time skepticism or fear of threat had been felt among the nation's middle and professional classes. Historian Jackson Lears has made an extensive study of American culture across the late nineteenth and early twentieth centuries, and finds a pervasive disquiet among the late-Victorian bourgeois in the midst of increasing immigration, in-dustrialization, and secularization. By the close of the nineteenth century, Lears reveals the nation's social fabric had begun to wear; official optimism had begun to flag. "Among educated Americans there was a growing sense of dis-ease." This growing perception among the educated and middle classes on the limita-tions of modernity created "a crisis of cultural authority," which grew out of *the social and psychic turmoil* of that unique time.[31] Public outcry against the social upheavals of the day from the educated and professional classes caused a wider skepticism among the masses. As we examine journalistic exposes, song lyrics, photo-essays, and nightly newscasts across the 1960s, we will find a similar dis-ease at play three-quarters of a century after late-Victorians experienced their own crisis of cultural authority, although concern in the late 1960s arose from a broader community than what anyone would characterize as uniquely middle-class bourgeois. The 1960s' conflagration of urban riots, racial antagonism, anti-war protest, counterculture dismissal of traditional middle-class values, and questions of political legitimacy created the cultural landscape from which we examine the rise of historic preservation and commemoration of a more heroic collective identity.

By examining the cultural landscape and the material culture contained within, we gain enormous insight into the mechanism of historic preservation and commemoration, and the social and psychic bases for and implications of these processes. We read the cultural landscape of the 1960s and what was imagined as a *better* landscape in order to more fully understand the role of commemoration and preservation of the past and why these were critical not only to the development of a city, but to the development of *a society*. Societal values, ideals, and norms that do not appear in the written historical record are often revealed in the cultural landscape. Much of society and culture operates from a subconscious level; we don't always spell it out. The father of material culture studies, Jules Prown, states what may appear obvious and yet must be made clear in order to fully appreciate what is at stake in the process of historic preservation, which is fundamentally the preservation of material culture from another era:

> The underlying premise is that human-made objects reflect, con-sciously or unconsciously, directly or indirectly, the beliefs of the individuals who commissioned, fabricated, purchased, or used them and, by extension, the beliefs of the larger society to which these indi-viduals belonged...Underlying cultural assumptions.... are detectable in the way things are said, or done, or made – that is, in their style.[32]

We study material culture – what folks create and leave behind - to discover the values and attitudes, often unspoken, of a particular society at a particular time and we do so from the cultural context of our own time. Therefore, when a Federalist style sloped-roof building is admired and restored for its aesthetic appeal in 1967, or when a sailing ship from the mid-nineteenth century is relocated to an East River landing in 1969 and restored to its former glory, we must understand that all of this restoration and re-creation has less to do with the physical structure of architecture or object of material culture and more certainly to do with the need to resuscitate a value system and mode of living wanting in the present condition. Where Victorian era bourgeois found heroism and dignity in the mythical warrior, represented through *objects d'art* of the Orient and from antiquity, South Street Seaport preservationists found in the mighty sea captain and brawny sailor of the mid-nineteenth century. In both cases, the social disorder of the day proved an unsatisfactory climate in which to locate heroism. The true hero was to be found elsewhere.

What the warrior represented to the bourgeois in 1900, the mariner represented to a growing cadre of preservation supporters at New York's South Street in the late 1960s: authentic selfhood, wholeness of purpose, and intensity of experience. The simplest way to realize our deepest values and ideals is by *acting out.* That is, by engaging in activities, which on the surface simply amuse us, we are actually "demonstrating in action the values by which we live."[33] The work of historic preservation, the work of restoring a square-rigger ship alongside an East River dock, of sailing schooners and romancing the sea, each *demonstrate in action the values by which one lives.* Historic preservation during this era embodied a social and personal regeneration for a generation – or two – seeking inspiration and uplift in the midst of a contentious cultural landscape: the Age of Sail represented an era when we were strong and good, during the disquieting dawning of the Age of Aquarius.

Chapter 1

POSTWAR PASTORAL; MILLER, MUMFORD AND RETHINKING MODERNISM

*I know full well that great cities are cursed with great
vices. The worst specimens of the human character,
squalid poverty, gorgeous, thoughtless luxury, misery and
anxiety, are all to be found in them. But we find, at
the same time, the noblest and most virtuous specimens
of our race on the same busy, bustling theatre.*

— *THOMAS RODERICK DEW (1836)*

When you think about historic preservation in New York City in the
1960s, at the forefront appears the staggering demolition of Penn
Station, images of its marble eagles unceremoniously dumped into the New
Jersey meadowlands. You think about Jane Jacobs and her public battles
against the city's icon of urban development, Robert Moses. You might turn
to Greenwich Village and the planned Lower Manhattan Expressway, and
the outcry from Jacobs and her cadre of supporters, intent on protecting the
uniquely twisted streets of the West Village from modernist urban planning that would cut right through the quieter cityscape. You might then ask

yourself, how many other interesting and historic structures were lost to the demands of urban expansion and renewal? You might try to take an inventory in your mind of the buildings the city has lost, and the buildings the city has saved.

But historic preservation in lower Manhattan in the 1960s was about much more than salvaging nineteenth century bricks and mortar, or challenging the proliferation of steel and glass superblocks transforming the city's skyline, or maintaining the more "human scale" of Federalist-era architecture. Beyond the well-studied Jane Jacobs-Robert Moses debates on the physical reconfiguration of the city and what that meant for its commercial development as well as its livability, the postwar historic preservation movement amounted to the resuscitation of a mythical, more noble collective identity in the midst of myriad challenges to American identity and the status quo. In fact, the process of re-creating and commemorating the city's preindustrial past served as a mechanism to reconnect with a more heroic collective identity and inspire better citizens. The restoration of carefully chosen vestiges of the urban landscape were meant to evoke memories of a glorious past and remind the public of America's origin myths during a time of social, cultural, and political upheaval.

Postwar era historic preservation in the urban landscape has been primarily explored, and explained, as a reaction against the bleakness of aesthetically uninspired modernist architecture, and the urban renewal bulldozer's utter transformation of the cityscape. The tearing down of New York's Pennsylvania Station in 1963 galvanized supporters of historic preservation and led to the passing of the City's Landmarks Preservation Law in 1965. This is certainly one side of the story, but this is not the entire story. Historic preservation and heritage commemoration in the 1960s served as a mechanism, like the earlier Colonial revival architectural movement and the American folk music revival, to shore up cultural authority during an era fraught with domestic civil strife and an increasingly questionable foreign war.

In order to fully appreciate the subtext underlying the work of historic preservation and heritage commemoration, we need to look at the movement as one sprung from two equally compelling paradigms. First, we must examine the history of *antimodern* sentiment in American culture. Since the onset of the Industrial Revolution, *the machine* has come to represents the physical manifestation of modern society; the machine equals progress and ingenuity. However, with the machine's incessant encroachment into all aspects of human activity, many writers, intellectuals, and artists have called for a rejection of the amoral machine in favor of a more noble, pastoral idyll. Thus, historic preservation in the postwar era must be understood as part of this longer trajectory of dis-ease and dissatisfaction with the modern urban condition. This impulse was not unique to the 1960s, although the circumstances of the 1960s were challenging in very unique and specific ways.

Second, we must understand historic preservation and heritage commemoration at New York City's seaport district as an effort to resuscitate the cultural authority of a "different breed of men" who seeded the city's early prosperity during a more heroic – real or otherwise - Age of Sail. These maritime-inspired origin myths, illuminated through early twentieth century histories on the port of New York as well as through art and literature, created imagery and collective memories of a time *when we were good,* and were part of a larger conversation surrounding the fundamental values and ideals of the nation's identity amidst an increasingly contested social and political landscape.

In his study of the American folk music revival, *When We Were Good; The Folk Revival,* historian Robert Cantwell recalls his generation's collective feeling of "apocalyptic dread" during the Cuban Missile Crisis and the mounting tension of the Cold War. The larger political and social realities – and horrific possibilities - of the Cold War, a burgeoning dread "so deep, prolonged and pervasive that it had become unconscious," moved a generation of young people towards a lyrical idyll that offered an otherwise powerless youth the opportunity to experience strength and solidarity through the often rebellious spirit of folk music.[34] For a slightly older generation experiencing the fragmentation and social upheaval of the 1960s, the historic preservation movement offered many of the same antidotes to a troubling modern condition that Cantwell finds through music.

Understood in light of these two prevailing themes – an antimodern sentiment and an attempt to resuscitate a collective cultural authority – historic preservation at New York's old seaport district was about much more than restoring slope-roofed buildings and square-rigger ships, or populating small shops with tradesmen and artisans, or providing a commercial boost to a stagnant local economy. Preserving the built environment of the "stirring times in the days of old, when the entire business and social life of the community centered on the toe of Manhattan Island" would remind visitors to South Street of an American identity steeped in heroic roots and national pride.[35] This message was critical during an era of violent contention and cultural upheaval, as a means to reinforce origin myths, secure collective identities, and create better citizens. Long before modernist architecture and federally funded urban renewal brought down the hammer on the jumbled hodge-podge of the nineteenth century cityscape, artists, writers, and urbanists have noted with alarm the impact of modernism on the human condition.

PASTORALISM IN THE NINETEENTH CENTURY

Since the eighteenth century, artists and intellectuals have sounded alarm at *the machine's* denigration of traditional culture. Freidrich Schiller in 1795 cautioned against the machine's nefarious ability to fracture man and society, while Thomas Carlyle accused modern technology of threatening man's "pure moral nature" and "true dignity of soul and character."[36] Adding to this rage against the machine, Charles Fraser wrote in 1846 that steam power "seems destined, in its future action and developments, to disturb *the moral economy* of the world by opposing that great law of the universe, which makes labor the portion of man, and condemns him to earn his bread by the sweat of his brow." In more modern writings, a nostalgia for the lost idyll of preindustrial America is evident from Herman Melville to Henry Miller, whose works focus on the "trope of the interrupted idyll" – modernity's booming, disquieting noise cutting through the serene landscape of the American wilderness.[37]

This collective appreciation for the return to a pastoral idyll in the midst of increasing technologies is loaded with morality judgment, in which the agrarian world is seen as a virtuous and morally superior aesthetic in contrast to the urban and industrial forces that threaten to destroy it. In *Machine in the Garden,* first published in 1964, Leo Marx argues the process of industrialization was the most critical event in American history, spurring a shift away from a predominantly agrarian society to an urban and industrial one. Marx reads the literary works of various artists across the American centuries as antennas of the age, in this way using literature as a window into the more elusive aspects of cultural change. Does art imitate life, or does life imitate art? Art, including the art of literature, speaks to the intangible aspects of culture, and Marx's astute analysis of literature across the centuries seeks to uncover these more elusive veins of societal shifts.

Marx's contribution to present-day understandings of antimodern sentiment in the American cultural landscape is important as a seminal work of cultural history in which Marx puts literary and artistic representations of culture at the center of his analysis. As part of the American Studies boom of the 1950s, Marx's cultural approach to history highlights the rise of American Studies during that decade and its concerns with the contradictions and conflicting ideals imbedded in American culture.[38] Marx-as-social-critic provides "a commentary on the American social and cultural landscape through the lens of literature, working under the premise that literature reflects the society from which it comes."[39] Marx's symbolic representation of a machine in a garden exposes for his reader the internal conflict between idealized myth and the present reality. Marx's argument, that the conflict of the machine in the garden is *the* central conflict in the American cultural experience, rests upon a single dialectic: the conflict between the pastoral ideal and technology. Some critics have faulted Marx's reliance on this single dialectic at the expense of other equally compelling conflicts, such as slavery and the Civil War, westward expansion, and cultural imperialism.[40]

Whether or not Marx successfully defends his thesis that there is a single dialectic which can describe the American cultural experience is a concern for another historian. For our purposes, Marx's primary contribution to our understanding of antimodern sentiment in the American intellectual and cultural landscape rests in *his search for a usable past* in the 1950s and '60s. Marx searches the past in order to answer questions in his own time, and for this we look to his work as evidence of mid-century concerns surrounding technology and modernity. That is, *Machine in the Garden* provides for us a window into American myth-making during Marx's own era. Further, Marx-as-social-activist intended his work to spur a larger national debate over the increasingly ubiquitous role of technology in the mid-century.[41] Marx's approach - tracing the development of a single cultural concept across several centuries - reveals to us his own concern, and the concern among certain intellectuals and cultural critics, of the encroachment of technology not during the eighteenth and nineteenth centuries, but during Marx's own time. As such, *Machine in the Garden* determines *for us* the significance of antimodern thought in the 1950s and '60s.[42] Concerned with the crisis of technology and the cultural tension this creates, Marx reveals to the contemporary reader a disquieting unrest as modernity and technology continued to advance across the American mid-century.

Urban historian Thomas Bender explores intellectual and institutional reactions to the nineteenth century's rise of industrialism and its effects on American cultural life. Bender uncovers a shift in American intellectual thought across the nineteenth century, in which the previously held Jeffersonian ideal of the "good citizen" who lives and works in the country ceded ideological territory to the realization that America's cultural and political life was increasingly tied to the growth of its cities. For better or for worse. By the mid-nineteenth century, Bender argues, Americans wanted it all: the moral fortification of the natural hinterland *as well as* the advances won by modern science and urban civilization.

Not all modern writers, surely, have viewed progress as disruptive or damaging to man's moral nature. In the vein of Manifest Destiny, many writers and artists of the modern age have appreciated *progress* as a formidable aspect of America's very birthright. While *Machine in the Garden* uncovers nineteenth century rhetoric on both sides of the technology debate, it is critical to note that arguments on both sides focused on the effects of technology on man's morality and virtue, for good or for bad. This point is critical: commentary on modern technology and scientific progress has been intricately laced with morality judgments and concerns for man's virtuosity. We do not simply quantify the appearance of technology and scientific progress in the American landscape; the emergence and proliferation of these invoke morality judgments as to how the latest technological innovation will affect the soul of man. The tools of modernity can either makes us, or break us. There is little neutrality, and each of Marx's author-subjects engages with this debate surrounding the machine's impact on humanity.

In the early nineteenth century, the locomotive emerged as the primary symbol of this disruption caused by the machine in the garden. The startling noise of the locomotive engine disrupts the psyche and causes profound alienation. Never before had human beings suffered such audible onslaught! By the 1830s, the locomotive had become a national obsession, an instrument of never-before-seen power, speed and noise. The locomotive presented "a sudden, shocking intruder upon a fantasy of idyllic satisfaction," where its brute masculine force disrupts the tranquil landscape before it.[43] As a prelude to the oncoming brave new world of total industrialization, the locomotive, with its explosive fire, iron and smoke, symbolized the seismic shift from agrarian to industrial society. The locomotive neatly embodies the transformative shift from the Age of Sail, to the Age of Steam and Steel, for at the center of that transformation was power and noise.

Many intellectuals of the nineteenth century certainly embraced scientific and technological innovations of the industrializing nation in conjunction with an appreciation for the natural world. The emergence of the machine in the garden was not systematically met with disapproval or consternation. One did not necessarily have to choose the machine *or* the garden. Men like John James Audubon, Frederick Law Olmsted, Ralph Waldo Emerson, Herman Melville, and Walt Whitman held an appreciation for scientific progress *and* for man's humanistic heritage. The ideals were not necessarily mutually exclusive. Olmsted, leader of the mid-nineteenth century's Parks movement and designer of both Manhattan's Central Park and Brooklyn's Prospect Park, believed in the power of great works of art and cultivated natural landscapes to exact a civilizing influence on the urban population. Olmsted felt the romance of art and nature would act as a refining influence on the disorderly and rather individualistic nature of American society.[44] This ideal - that nature, art and the teachings of humanism would create better citizens, that a romantic or pastoral landscape harbored the moral power to calm the soul and uplift the citizenry - was the guiding force behind the Parks movement. For Olmsted, the city park – complete with rural landscaping and public monuments – created a breeding ground for civic-minded, democratic ideals and would create better citizens. The very creation of a park was meant to provide a contemplative and contented oasis for the urban dweller as an individual, and for urban society writ large.

Steeped in an ideology of environmental determinism, the Parks movement, like the City Beautiful movement that would reach its height of aesthetic and symbolic appeal a few decades later, relied heavily on a trust in the physical environment's ability to shape one's character. That is, to the nineteenth century urbanist, the environment must be structured via grandiose architecture and cultivated green spaces in order to make better citizens of the immigrant masses and the poor. Public monuments, classical architecture, and the cultivated landscaping of green spaces in Central and Prospect Parks combined to impart a very distinct sense of cultural authority and impart moral values. These were aesthetic projects meant to influence the constant flux of urban residents and to bolster the creation of good citizens.

The American response to modernization and to cities themselves is ripe with competing arguments directed at both the glory and vices of urbanization. Thomas Roderick Dew, of The College of William and Mary, likened the grandeur of certain northeastern American cities to that of ancient Egypt, Rome, and China. Wrote Dew:

> I know full well that great cities are cursed with great vices. The worst specimens of the human character, squalid poverty, gorgeous, thoughtless luxury, misery and anxiety, are all to be found in them. But we find, at the same time, the noblest and most virtuous specimens of our race on the same busy, bustling theatre. It is the cities which have hurried forward the great revolution of modern times, "whether for weal or woe." It is the cities which have made the great improvements and inventions in mechanics and the arts. It is the great

cities which have pushed every department of literature to the highest pitch of perfection. It is the great cities alone which can build up and sustain hospitals, asylums, dispensaries -which can gather together large and splendid libraries, form literary and philosophical associations, assemble together banks of literati, who stimulate and encourage each other. In fine, it is the large cities alone which can rear up and sustain a mere literary class.[45]

Clearly, *antimodern* is neither a particularly helpful nor definitive characterization of the way we think about cities, unless we understand this term does not simply entail a derision of modernity, but encompasses a more complicated view on the *problematic changes* associated with the modernizing city. We must further consider that by the turn of the twentieth century, Progressive Era antimodernism became an increasingly specific response to the cultural landscape *at that time.* American cultural historian Jackson Lears argues these antimodern dissenters retreated from the increasing pervasiveness of industrialization and instead sought antidotes in the perceived purity of Oriental and other native cultural productions.[46] Like Marx, Lears notes an acute subtext of morality judgment fundamental to antimodernist thought, and finds Progressive Era middle- and upper-class nostalgia for moral and spiritual renewal a very specific response to the perceived immoral effects of industrial technology. This nostalgia was felt primarily among the educated and affluent middle and upper-classes, a nostalgia not simply laced with escapism, but stemming from a complex ambivalence which involved both an appreciation for material progress *and* the luxury of sentimentality.[47] That is, this nostalgia sprung from a very specific bourgeoisie privilege in which one both appreciated modern conveniences and lamented the loss of a perceived primitive authenticity these conveniences displaced.

Lears is careful to explain that late-Victorian dissenters were not against modernity so much as increasingly aware of the problems, limitations, and contradictions associated with progress. This turn-of-the-century antimodernism was not simply concurrent with the tumultuous industrial landscape of the era, but that turmoil was in fact *the basis* for antimodern dissent. Cultural ferment, challenges to the traditional order, an influx of immigration, and heightened urban change fueled tensions and created longings for a better version of a preindustrial American society. Through its very core, turn-of-the-century antimodern sentiment, in all its forms, was a mechanism used by the ruling class to retain cultural authority and sense of control amidst an unruly social, economic, and political climate.[48]

Antimodernism, therefore, is not simply a cry against the modern urban condition, and should not be understood as such. Instead, antimodernism should be understood as *an awareness of a dis-ease* associated with industrialization, capitalism, technological progress, and urbanism. By the turn-of-the-century, late-Victorian fears related to issues of race and class, immigration, the urban problem, and the social question lead to a sense of social disorder that made the bourgeoisie quite nervous.[49] Sensing burgeoning social chaos and a "crisis of cultural authority" over the physical and moral decay of the nation's cities, the spread of science and rational technology into all aspects of daily living, and the decreasing value placed on previously held religious tenets, the ruling classes of the late-Victorian era found themselves in the midst of a spiritual and cultural transformation. Indeed, these antimodern impulses were steeped in a nostalgic yearning to grab hold of a cultural landscape quickly vanishing from the modern scene.[50]

Part of this longing looked adoringly upon the work of the premodern artisan, the man who worked with his hands. The decades surrounding 1900 witnessed the Arts and Crafts Movement and a revival of handicrafts, prized primarily among the educated bourgeoisie, the class most concerned with this crisis of cultural authority. For it was the bourgeoisie professional and business class, arguably, whose position had become most tenuous and vulnerable amidst the social upheavals of the day.[51] The threat of massive change in the prevailing social structure, in the cultural landscape, and in the hegemonic order created a collective sense of nostalgia for a more authentic way of life when power structures were more firmly rooted in place.

THE CRISIS OF TECHNOLOGY IN THE TWENTIETH CENTURY

By the dawn of the twentieth century, new discoveries in science and technology, deeply entrenched in Darwinism and emerging race theory, produced a conviction among Progressive Era reformists and urbanists that social engineering, steeped in environmental determinism, was the key to orderly development of the chaotic industrial city. Immigration, disorder, and chaos also characterized cities of the mid-nineteenth century; an understanding of the city as fragmented, diverse and contentious was not new to twentieth century urbanists. The difference, however, between nineteenth century perceptions of a city divided and those that would dominate the twentieth century is found in the earlier expectation that fragmentation would last only a generation or two. Environmental determinism grew out of the central tenet that a careful molding of the physical and cultural landscape – which included not only the structures in which urban dwellers lived, worked and played, but also addressed cultural practices like child rearing, personal hygiene, and religious practices – was exorbitantly influential on individual and group behavior. The legacy of this ideology of environmental determinism will not go unnoticed in the resurgence of historic preservation in the 1960s.

Progressive reform ideals were heavily influenced by transnational ideologies, as global interdependency and discourse on how to attend to the urban problem crossed both sides of the Atlantic in response to rapid urbanization, the effects of unregulated industrialization and the resulting social crisis.[52] While the urbanistic impulse during the Progressive Era appears one of hope and optimism for a cleaner, safer, more rational environment, reformist concerns surrounding the state of America's industrial cities were steeped in an understanding of the modern city as *essentially* chaotic and disorderly, in need of rational planning and humane direction.

A "canary in a coalmine" describes an early warning sign of danger. The artist frequently represents the leading public voice of challenge to the status quo, presenting a visual or literary manifestation of his acute perceptions on the life he witnesses and experiences; a canary in a coalmine. Artistic and cultural representations, therefore, constitute a critical form of evidence in any analysis of American cities and perspectives on the modern urban experience. Since the early twentieth century, scholars and artists alike have characterized the modern American experience as an *urban* experience, and yet responses to the urban condition across the century have tended to represent the city as dysfunctional. From Theodore Dreiser's *Sister Carrie*, to Nathan West's *Day of the Locust,* to Richard Wright's "The Man Who Lived Underground," to Henry Miller's *Air Conditioned Nightmare*, to Don DeLillo's *Underworld*, to Philip Roth's *American Pastoral*, to T.C. Boyle's *Tortilla Curtain*... there exists no end to the literary canon exploring the contentious urban experience. From the Progressive Era through Modernism and into the Postmodern age, artists and scholars of urbanism have expressed a marked dis-ease with the urban landscape in its *present condition*. While the city might embody the spirit of opportunity and represent a critical site of intellectual and cultural life for diverse communities – an ideal that illuminates the "triumph of the city" - the growth of this organism known as The City must not go unchecked.[53]

Historian Thomas Bender suggests the American city can be culturally represented in two allegorical forms, which he dubs the "City of Ambition" and the "City of Making Do."[54] While the "City of Ambition," *appears* glossy and triumphant, these devilish entrapments are merely superficial and are meant to temporarily obscure an urban reality that is disarming, alienating, often fatal. Written at the turn-of-the-century, Theodore Drieser's *Sister Carrie* neatly represents the "City of Ambition." Here, Drieser depicts Chicago and New York City as sites of possibility and potential, while the reader soon finds the cities riddled with darkness and despair. Both the reader and Drieser's characters quickly understand that the city is where you make it or lose it; lives are remarkably improved or fatally destroyed. The city is hypnotic, the lure of its influence irresistible. Dreiser offers no real reason for his character Hurstwood's downfall; this is simply how it goes in the Big City of capitalist consumption. Sister Carrie rises, and Hurstwood falls. Much like Edward Bellamy's *Looking Backward From 2000 to 1887*, in which a well-to-do protagonist suddenly awakens to find himself located in a socialist nightmare one hundred and thirteen years hence, Dreiser warns that a tantalizingly modern, comfortable lifestyle is dangerously tenuous in the capitalist system; it could all be gone in an instant.[55]

Bender's "The City of Making Do" offers a counter-representation to this "City of Ambition." Ashcan School artists, led by Philadelphian John Sloan, portrayed the social and economic inequalities of urban life with an entirely new focus on vernacular life in the city, its sidewalks and streets. Sloan's visual work helped create a collective image of urban life in the American consciousness; the work of Ashcan artists documents the lives of ordinary people on the urban scene, thus engaging the viewer through a new eye-level perspective.[56] The work of Ashcan School artists such as John Sloan and Everett Shinn, along with the later 1920s paintings of muralist Reginald Marsh, represent visually the social and political dynamism of a city in flux. These artists' streetscapes alternate in temperament and feeling between the vitality of the evening rush hour - as depicted in John Sloan's *Six O'Clock Winter*, which captures the busy end to a busy day for appropriately-dressed New Yorkers who have just completed an industrious day of work, shopping, or other urban pursuit - to Everett Shinn's *Eviction*, which offers a somber portrayal of an unfortunate family, downcast eyes and banished to the streets, their belongings still in the process of removal from what was once home. The city can offer opportunity and interaction, or dejection and desolation. In either case, and applicable to all scenarios in between, the city must be reckoned with.

The urban dynamism captured in these early twentieth century works of art reappears in Hollywood musicals such as *On the Town* and *42nd Street*, which depict the best cinematic representations of the city. Here, New York City is portrayed as open, receptive and fascinating. These films, however, are not concerned with social realism or criticism, rather "stylizing and mythologizing the social universe so an audience could escape" into a romantic fantasy. These films add to the city-mythmaking of an otherwise contentious urban landscape. In the 1970s and '80s, Woody Allen's films provide an antidote to artistic representations of urban madness which can be traced back to the earliest dystopian films such as *Metropolis*, *The City*, and film noir, and those that predominate Allen's own era, such as *Death Wish*, *Taxi Driver*, *Escape from New York*, *Midnight Cowboy*, *Chinatown*, *Saturday Night*

Fever, and *Blade Runner*. Allen's is a city of promise, possibility and grandeur, populated by a Manhattan-centric upper middle class cast of characters. Films like *Manhattan* represent the collective memory of Old New York, a mythical ideal of the old *city on the hill*, a fantasy similar to the stylized cityscape of the old Hollywood musicals.[57]

While these paintings and films are very specifically situated in New York City, the effect these and other cultural representations of Gotham have had on the conceptualization of American cities in the public realm cannot be overstated. For much of the twentieth century, New York – more than any other city - dominated public conceptions of the modern American metropolis: complex, diverse, full of artifice and cause for suspicion.[58] While today's scholars and artists understand that no unified conceptual understanding of *the city* exists, cultural representations of New York City do point to larger trends in American cultural consciousness as to the symbolism of the modern urban condition. For better of for worse, cultural depictions of the Empire City have informed a collective sense of modern urban life for well over a century.

Literature across the early-to-mid twentieth century, which speaks to the dysfunction of American urban and industrial society in the 1930s, '40s and '50s, is ripe with antimodern sentiment and reflects a simmering malaise in the public consciousness. Underworld literature of the 1930s and '40s reflects a moral panic over the urban environment: racial strife, immigration and the urban masses as an unstoppable organism. Assimilation and the enculturation of immigrant populations had not, as Progressive reformers anticipated, proceeded in an orderly and rational manner. In response to continued social contestation, themes of the underworld predominate literature, photography, and film. Now, not only is the city understood as an organism, so are the masses who inhabit it. The chaotic impulse of the crowd dominates dystopian writings and film noir, in which the struggle between man, nature and the urban machine creates a gritty urban landscape.

American writer and social critic Henry Miller's *The Air-Conditioned Nightmare* protests against all that is wrong with the industrial landscape of modern America. Perhaps no other literary figure of the mid-century so clearly bemoans and finds horror with the condition of the American urban scene. Miller returned to the United States in 1939, after ten years living abroad as an expatriate in Paris and Greece. He undertook a year-long, ten-thousand-plus mile trek around the U.S. in 1940, the experiences from which he wrote and then published his book in 1945. Miller's journey began on a steamship from Greece to New York City, stopping first in Boston. Miller had hoped to like Boston. Instead, he was grossly disappointed and saddened by what he viewed upon his arrival. He did not like the look or feel of the mid-century American house, which appeared barren, cold, and harsh. American architecture was not in any way pleasing to our writer. Not only the architecture, but the Boston *mob* nauseated Miller, who was happy to leave port as soon as possible. Miller's characterization of New York City rates no better: "I felt as I had always felt about New York- that it is the most horrible place on God's earth."⁵⁹

Having lived abroad the previous decade, Miller observed upon his 1939 return, "a great change had come over America, no doubt about that... Everything was cock-eyed, and getting more and more so... The lack of resilience, the feeling of hopelessness, the resignation, the skepticism, the defeatism... And over it all that same veneer of fatuous optimism – *only now decidedly cracked.*" Miller found mid-century American urban life loathsome, dull, monotonous, and terrifying. "Nowhere else in the world is the divorce between man and nature so complete."⁶⁰

From Pittsburgh, Miller writes "never has the status quo seemed more hideous to me." Our traveller describes gangs of armed brutes terrorizing the streets of Pittsburgh, men who looked ready to kill, slaughter, or maim without much provocation. While the amenities of Miller's hotel were admittedly nice enough, he found the air deadly, the city's spirit wretched. Miller describes flagging industrial towns of the Northeast – Pittsburgh, Youngstown, Detroit, Bayonne, Bethlehem, and Scranton -- as veritable wastelands. While the New Yorker admits he witnessed miseries and suffering in the South as well as the North, at least, he writes, he felt some peace in the South. Miller found the worst form of suffering in the country's North and East, where the push towards *progress* reigned supreme. This progress, the physical and social detritus of industrial capitalism, had wreaked havoc on the nation's natural beauty, with tract after tract of rich land transformed to wasteland. "Wherever there is industry there is ugliness, misery, oppression, gloom and despair."[61]

Miller locates America's golden age about one hundred years before his assessment of the state of the nation; a time, in fact, still dominated by sail over steam. Since that time, "everything that was of beauty, significance or promise has been destroyed and buried in the avalanche of false progress." The dreams and visions of Great Americans had, by 1945, crumbled and vanished. The poets and the seers of an earlier age had tried their best, but "some other breed of man has won out."[62]

E.B. White, frequent contributor of both sketch and prose to *The New Yorker* magazine throughout the mid-twentieth century, wrote in 1949 perhaps his most famous essay, "Here is New York." White, a one-time quintessential New Yorker, had by this time relocated with his wife, *The New Yorker's* literary editor Katharine Angell, to the cooler climes of North Brooklin, Maine. On his 1948 return – during an unbearable summer heat wave - White describes a city filled with possibility and even magic, but at the same time cramped and suffocating. The paradox of New York is that it is changeless, and yet constantly changing. Amidst White's appreciation for the city he clearly fell in love with years ago, a city "unique, cosmopolitan, mighty, and unparalleled," the reader senses more than a glimpse of sadness for what has been lost. "The city has never been so uncomfortable, so crowded, so tense." New York harbor, however, was one of White's bright observances, and he is pleased to cite its reputation, still, as one of the greatest seaports in the world.[63]

Urbanist and cultural critic Lewis Mumford, the leading authority on architecture and urbanism throughout much of the twentieth century, writes with caution on the increasing role of technology and the machine in all aspects of modern life in his 1967 book, *The Myth of the Machine*. What the locomotive symbolized for Nathaniel Hawthorne in the 1830s, the machine symbolized for Lewis Mumford by the 1960s. In his earlier writings, Mumford insisted the city was primarily a social construct, less a physical construction.[64] Heavily influenced by Patrick Geddes' *Cities in Evolution*, Mumford called for the decentralization of crowded industrial cities of "the old palaeotechnic order" during the height of 1920's urban density, to regional garden cites where humans could live more closely – and in better health - with nature. In the 1920s and '30s, Mumford worked closely with the Regional Planning Association, which called for the decentralization of over-crowded Eastern and Midwestern cities as a remediation for their inevitable and continued growth. By the 1960s, Mumford had become less focused on urban growth *per se* and was heavily concerned with the proliferation of the machine and *technics* – a term Mumford used widely to connote the iterative relationship between technological innovation and all aspects of a society's cultural milieu - into now every aspect of modern life.

The proliferation of technology over the course of a century had, by the American mid-century, exacerbated concerns about the brave new world of mechanization well beyond the warnings of Hawthorne and Progressive Era reformers. By the early 1960s, it was clear to artists and intellectuals alike that technology and mechanization now "dominated every aspect of our existence" and rendered many individuals across Western society "hyper-emotional and irrational," a sentiment Mumford equally abhorred.[65] Mumford provides literary evidence to man's historical resistance to the machine by citing romantic writers dating back to Bacon, Shakespeare, Goethe, Rousseau, and Hugo, each of whom attempted to place human activity at center stage "instead of accepting the machine as center and holding all its values to be final and absolute."[66] This romantic reaction against the machine manifested in three distinct forms: the cult of history, the cult of nature, and the cult of the primitive, each of which embodied an overreaction – hyper-emotional and irrational – to the encroachment of the machine into everyday life. Since the machine had complete disregard for place or past, the cult of history – and its offspring, the fetishization of history- emerged as a reaction to this disregard.

The cult of history and the cult of nature represent to Mumford something of an unwelcome romantic idyll, steeped in man's need to control the machine as he attempts to assert restraint on its ever-increasing presence.[67] These romantic, and, as Mumford argues, *irrational* responses are motivated by "the lure of more primitive conditions of life, as an alternative to the machine." Further, Mumford cautions this cult of history constitutes a "bedraggled retreat" from modern life, here echoing Sigmund Freud's amazement at the tendency of allegedly educated men to idealize and romanticize a primitive way of life.[68] Mumford finds this retreat absurd, cautioning "if such defeatism becomes widespread, it would mean something more than the collapse of the machine: it would mean the end of the present cycle of Western Civilization."[69]

By 1967, Mumford appears less critical of these emotional reactions against the machine, and becomes personally concerned that man is well on his way to becoming a machine-serving drone in the age of the Megamachine. In *The Myth and The Machine: Technics and Human Development*, Mumford reports technology is now completely disassociated from the larger cultural sphere of humankind and predicts things will go very badly in an age of increasing automation.[70] In the company of twentieth century writers like George Orwell, Aldous Huxley, Henry Miller, and Franz Kafka, Mumford too cautions that man cannot flourish as a cog in the industrial machine, reduced to a dreary and inorganic automaton.

MODERN MELANCHOLIA

Melancholy is nothing new. Albrecht Dürer's 1514 masterful engraving, "Melancholia I," is perhaps the most recognized and widely admired interpretation depicting this angst that plagues human dramas and fuels unwelcome feelings of yearning and regret. Tangled up with the increasing industrialization of our nation, Americans have long experienced a complicated and often uneasy relationship with modernity and the modernizing city; an alternate iteration, either past or future, is idealized. *Modern melancholia*: a melancholic yearning for the loss of the romanticized preindustrial past. Our dis-ease with the modern condition should not, however, come as a surprise. The present, by its very nature, is problematic because it neither lives up to our expectations of what a modern city should be, nor has it yet realized the idealized visions we hold for the future. Nostalgia, a sentimental yearning for that which never actually existed, colors many interpretations of the past, urban and otherwise.

Albrecht Dürer, "Melancholia I." Copper plate engraving, 1514.
No copyright permissions required, work created prior to 1923 is in the public
domain. Per Stanford University Libraries, "Copyright and Fair Use"

It is pointless to ask whether the new [cities] are better or worse than the old, since there is no connection between them, just as the old post cards do not depict [the old city] as it was, but a different city which, by chance, was called Maurilia, like this one.[71]

— ITALO CALVINO, *INVISIBLE CITIES* (1978)

Italian writer Italo Calvino proposes there is no real connection between the old city and the new, they simply share the same name and are located upon the same topographical landscape. *This* city is not *that* one. Calvino stresses the realities of the new city cannot possibly compensate for the imagined "lost grace" of the old, which is only really appreciated in the viewing of old postcards and was likely not particularly graceful to those who lived it.[72] The graceful old city *can be appreciated only as such in hindsight,* through picture postcards and the preservation of old buildings. We must remember that in its day, the old city did not appear especially graceful to its inhabitants, who were confronted with the gritty realities of the day, ranging from disease to political strife to religious persecution. We create these images of the past only from the cultural landscape of our present circumstance. The postcard city is the city of *our* dreams, the city as we wish to remember it and to know it.

WHEN WE WERE GOOD: THE COLONIAL REVIVAL

Clearly, a tradition exists in both scholarly and literary writings as to the disorienting effects of industrialization and the modern urban condition. We call this dissatisfaction *antimodernism,* but note this term represents less a stance against the progress associated with modernity and more acutely as a growing understanding of and concern for *the problematic and alienating nature of modern urban and technological society.* Modernity did not yield Utopia. Responses to these concerns manifest in a number of ways, including a growing nostalgia for a perceived lost idyll, a better version of American society located in the pastoral or preindustrial realm. Two cultural movements which bring to life this nostalgic look back to a better version of American society, to a time *when we were good,* include the Colonial Revival movement in architecture beginning in the 1870s, and the American folk music revival which grew steadily from the early 1900s. While on the surface, both movements were fueled by a nostalgic yearning for a "simpler," more *authentic* era, in subtler ways, they served to shore up cultural authority and collective identity in the face of challenge to the reigning status quo.

We must first understand the role that visual and material culture – including architecture and art - play in the creation of identity and memory. We need to know how and by whom memories are shaped for collective consumption; what do these collective memories attempt to legitimate? In the social landscape of the late nineteenth century, the Colonial revival in architecture was one such mechanism meant to identify and solidify the primacy of the nation's colonial heritage. Psychologist Mihaly Csikszentmihalyi explains humanity's psychological need for objects, answering why, among a variety of reasons, we need things. Csikszentmihalyi argues objects serve as totems, symbols of power. Objects are the physical manifestation of our often-unconscious ideals and value systems and help identify us to ourselves and to the outside world. In times of heightened social-political-cultural change, the use of objects as a means to shore up personal and collective identities intensifies.[73] The precariousness of societal change leads us to perceive objects as symbols of stability that provide meaning in an otherwise unruly cultural landscape. Buildings of a preferred architectural style, monuments commemorating idealized figures, and interior furnishings and objects d'art of a bygone era each serve this purpose of legitimizing cultural ideals because antiquity equals value, and what is preserved is remembered as valuable, while the rest is forgotten in its perceived insignificance.

Philosopher-writer Alain de Botton expands upon Csikszentmihalyi's theory of why we need things and includes the human need for recurring and positive reinforcement. Why are we so vulnerable to our surroundings? Why do we even ask our environment to speak to us, to influence our very mood? Beautiful objects – however we define the term – remind us of our highest ideals, and ground us in what we value and hold dear in the face of incessant dissatisfaction with the disappointments of life. Home is our refuge from the world, and what we admire in the architecture of home, we admire in the architecture of public buildings as well.

De Botton describes the myriad ways in which the built environments of our homes and workplaces have the ability to inspire or degrade our larger aspirations. We behave differently, for example, in a cathedral, a home, a disco; we are different people.[74] De Botton acknowledges the power of architecture lies simply in its ability to *suggest* a moral message or ideal, but has no power to enforce these. Like the steadfast belief in environmental determinism which dominated the social reform movement of the Progressive Era, de Botton argues architecture speaks to us and has the ability to alter the ways in which we confront a seemingly random and challenging world. Much in the same way that we read nonverbal cues from people, we read buildings and ascribe human attributes to them. "What we search for in a work of architecture is not in the end so far from what we search for in a friend. The objects we describe as beautiful are versions of the people we love."[75] Architecture, whether from the classical, gothic, baroque, or modernist periods, can *make us good* because something of the integrity and honesty of its origin– whether real or imagined – survives its creators and permeates the environment in which it remains. De Botton offers:

> It is perhaps when our lives are at their most problematic that we are likely to be most receptive to beautiful things. Our downhearted moments provide architecture and art with their best openings, for it is at such times that our hunger for their ideal qualities will be at its height.[76]

"When our lives are at their most problematic" is key. It is during times of disorder and dissent when we, as insecure human beings, most often seek comfort and strength in the solidity of objects. Immigration, industrialization, and social disorder following post-Civil War reconstruction characterized many cities of the mid-to-late nineteenth century. By the dawn of the twentieth century, new discoveries in science and technology, deeply entrenched in Darwinism and emerging race theory, produced a conviction among progressive reformists and urbanists that social engineering, steeped in environmental determinism, was the key to orderly development of the chaotic industrial city. Progressive Era reformists acknowledged the urban problem, raised the social question, and pushed for civilizing influences that would transform immigrant and ethnic populations into solid American citizens. With this new perspective on environmental determinism emerged the theory that material culture – including architecture, objects, and artifacts - held the power to *transform one's character.* Environmental determinism allows that simply being in the presence of colonial antiques could ennoble one's character, believing objects crafted by preindustrial tradesmen of the Colonial Era "embodied the superior values" of the day, represented the "spirit of the past," and, most critically, *transmitted the noble spirit of the past* to their new owners.[77] Late nineteenth century collectors of Colonial Era antiques felt these objects represented a better (if more stratified) version of American society, a time when:

> Social life was cultivated and enjoyed, and the distinctions of class were observed and acquiesced in…without any loss of self-respect or happiness to those who acknowledged the refined, the wealthy, and the intellectual superiority of others.[78]

Eliza Greatroix' 1875 assertion, reflecting her nostalgia for an era when "the distinctions of class were observed and acquiesced in" indicates what, exactly, was sentimentalized in the homage to all things colonial. By the end of the nineteenth century, amidst a large increase in immigration, post-Reconstruction migration, and a growing awareness that an urban problem demanded attention, material culture of the Colonial Era served as a reminder of an imagined American society in which folks allegedly "acknowledged the refined, the wealthy, and the intellectual superiority of others."

This was a firmly delineated class hierarchy, with the lower classes more solidly bound in place. By the end of the nineteenth century, objects and architecture of the Colonial Era represented, in addition to aesthetic tastes in interior wainscoting and exterior pillars, traditional class distinctions and social hierarchies. When de Botton tells us, "What we search for in a work of architecture is not in the end so far from what we search for in a friend," he argues a neoclassical pediment above an arched doorway is not simply aesthetically pleasing to its present-day admirer; its design evokes the character and values of those who dwelled there.

Patriotic sentiment fueled the Colonial revival from the 1870s through the 1950s, in which preserved and restored Colonial Era buildings were enobled by the connections these had with heroes and leaders of the Revolutionary War era.[79] The popular appeal of the Colonial style, to which the later revival harkened, was as much about patriotism and a national style distinct from European styles as it was about an architectural aesthetic. Horace Mann, architect and a member of the Sons of the Revolution, declared in 1915:

> There remains in our own Colonial or Georgian style... a real sense of ownership. It has grown up with the nation, and no more tangible expression of our national character could be found. There is between Americans and Europeans an actual difference of habit of mind. We are less complex and more direct, less formal and simpler, and all this our Colonial work expresses.[80]

The symbolism we associate with any architectural style is at least as important, if not more so, than its aesthetic appeal. The appreciation for the Colonial architectural style, then, is loaded with value judgments, just as in the pastoral ideal. The Colonial style represents a visible symbol of national character, distinct in both time and place. By the early twentieth century, the ongoing Colonial revival in architecture promoted the nation's *authentic* cultural origins and helped define a distinct American heritage in the midst of the First World War, economic depression, and socio-demographic flux. In the midst of challenging circumstances of national or regional proportion, the power of cultural representation, while perhaps not quite propaganda, serves to impart and solidify desired collective values.

By the 1930s, resurgence in American nationalism following the devastation of World War I and the Great Depression included a belief in the power of architecture to remind us of past values, of a simpler, purer, more manageable world.[81] Home décor magazines of the 1930s were filled with photographs and exposés on the Colonial-type home, and helped fuel a middle-class patriotic sentiment. In addition to magazines such as *House and Garden, Architecture,* and *House Beautiful,* Hollywood films fastidiously promoted the Colonial style, with almost every film of the 1930s set upon a Colonial-style suburban backdrop.[82] While home interior design of the 1930s evoked an idealized vision of the colonial past, it simultaneously took full advantage of modern conveniences, the latest technological gadgets, and home appliances. We don't want to actually *live* in an antique home, we simply want to create the aura of one with all the comforts of the modern age, available to middle-class consumers through home-delivery catalogues like Lillian Vernon and Sears & Roebuck.

The popularity of Colonial Williamsburg sparked an already lively colonial-inspired historic preservation fixation across the 1930s. The park's 1937 guidebook cites the patriotic and inspirational benefits of historic preservation during the "topsy-turvy times" of the Great Depression and the spread of "anti-democratic" forces at home.[83] Industrialist John D. Rockefeller, Jr. meant to instill the lessons of patriotism and commemoration of our nation's forefathers when he first laid plans to recreate the colonial village at Williamsburg. Not everyone was a fan, however, and among the dissenters was the modernist architect Frank Lloyd Wright, who characterized Colonial Williamsburg as a "hangover," indicating "a mawkish sentimentality for a past that wasn't any good."[84] Wright's comments challenge the *historical amnesia* quality of these restoration/preservation projects: What of history is omitted? What in fact is being preserved or restored? Who comes out ahead in the commemoration of a selective version of history?

If we detect a certain amount of xenophobia in the motivations behind the Colonial revival movement, we would not be misguided. The subtext of the Colonial revival, in which the popular consumption of Colonial Era architecture and décor serves to shore up the cultural authority of an Anglo-white middle class which feels itself threatened by immigration, the Great Migration of southern African-Americans into the north, and an increasingly multi-ethnic population, has been criticized as a mechanism for maintaining the status quo. Colonial style and the symbolism ascribed to it were associated with the heritage of the nation's forefathers, a strong foundation in family life, and a keener religious sensibility. Because the prevailing social order was potentially threatened by these social-demographic shifts, architectural and material "cornerstones" of the nation's colonial foundation became especially significant. "By resorting to bygone modes, these groups strove to preserve their sense of the nation's beginnings, to maintain traditions, and *to make the present less threatening.*"[85]

Memory is constructed, not reproduced, through a process by which we reshape our understandings of the past to fit present-day concerns. We tend to construct a mythologized and stable past in response to the troublesome and threatening changes in the present. Understood in this light, a cultural ideal as apparently benign as an architectural style becomes loaded with value judgments of authenticity and purity. The Colonial revival appealed to the middle-class as a way to legitimate links to the past and provided a sense of roots – real or imaginary - amidst challenges to the status quo during the height of industrialization, immigration, and urbanization. Similar efforts to retain cultural authority during times of social turbulence are seen in the folk music revival of the early-mid 1900s, and again in the resurgence of the historic preservation movement amidst the social turbulence of the 1960s.

WHEN WE WERE GOOD: THE AMERICAN FOLK MUSIC REVIVAL

Come on all you exploited workingmen
And fight for Freedom's cause,
For you are bound, both hand and foot
By capitalistic laws;
Your voices you can raise no more,
Your lips you now must steal,
For if you rise to speak a word
A gun-man's at your heel.

— *"ORGANIZE" BY JAMES FERRITER (1919). AMERICAN FOLK SONG*

It is critical that we avoid making the generalization that heritage commemoration in any era necessarily privileges one class or community at every turn. In the case of the Colonial revival in architecture, a white Anglo tradition belonging to the founding families of the Colonial Era was idealized as noble, honest and good. In the case of the folk music revival, what began at the turn of the twentieth century as a celebration of the hegemonic cultural authority of the Scotch-English descendants in Appalachian communities had morphed, by the 1930s, to a celebration of "ordinary folk" idealized as noble, honest and good in their struggles to stay afloat during the Depression, and would morph yet again by the 1960s. These revivals in architecture and music were steeped in notions of heroism, with the former locating heroism in the traditions of the nation's patriotic founding families, and the latter locating heroism in the strength of ordinary folk, often marginalized, but standing for the best of "American values."[86] Both traditions sought to honor a time *when we were good,* promoting an overt, and sometimes covert, value system seemingly lacking in the present cultural landscape.

The American folk music revival dates to the early twentieth century, when American folk music collectors began forming state folklore societies. These primarily academic collectors meant to catalogue and preserve America's folk heritage through traditional ballads and vernacular music not corrupted by the popular music of modern society.[87] Englishman Cecil Sharp, an authority on British folk songs, travelled to America's Appalachian region in 1916, where he recovered and collected over sixteen hundred versions of five hundred songs, eventually publishing these in *English Folk Songs from the Southern Appalachians* the following year. Sharp intended to replace the popular music of the day with traditional Anglo folk songs that had survived within these insulated mountain communities. He wanted to "flood the street with folk tunes" and displace the cacophony of "coarse music-hall songs," thereby making "the streets a pleasanter place for those who have sensitive ears." This, Sharp believed, would do "incalculable good" for the still-uncivilized masses."[88] In the early twentieth century era of environmental determinism, folk music - like the contemporaneous City Beautiful and Colonial revival movements in architecture - was seen as a civilizing influence on the public, offered as an antidote to the chaos created by modern music in a modern society.

By the early twentieth century, traditional middle and ruling-class culture was being challenged on several fronts, including expanding commercialization, secularization, urbanization, and industrial capitalism. From this troublesome cultural landscape, Sharp imagined and helped to create an idealized vision of folk culture through recovered folk music. Sharp presented this folk culture for popular consumption as natural and wholesome, in marked contrast to what he described as the spiritual vacuum of modern industrial society. Appalachian life – to the outsider, if not to those who lived it - was decidedly better, more authentic, and pure. Folk music represented a mountain people immune to the grinding pressure of the modern, urban world. With his marketing of folk music as the true musical heritage of the nation, Sharp sentimentalized the preindustrial culture of "ordinary" mountain folk.[89]

Sharp's interest in reviving American folk music contained more than a hint of supercilious racism; his project centered on legitimizing the specifically Anglo heritage of American culture. By choosing Appalachia for his study, he chose a relatively ethnically homogeneous region, one in which Anglo descendants - themselves the children of immigrants - were often impoverished and illiterate. This was a revival seeking not the idyll of a longed-for past, but the idyll of a past which never actually occurred. In Sharp's implication that *traditional* American culture was a white Anglo-Saxon culture and the nation's true "authentic" heritage, the emergence of the folk music revival underscores a mechanism similar to that at play during the Colonial revival. The 1910s mark a decade when racial boundaries across the country were pushed, with increasing immigration from southern and eastern Europe and the first Great Migration of African-Americans creating widespread demographic shifts in the nation's urban centers. Sharp's vision of the folk revival – located in rural Appalachia - intended to shore up America's "authentic" heritage against potential challenges from other cultural and ethnic groups.[90]

To be sure, not all folk music collectors focused solely on English folk songs and their white singers. African-American spirituals were becoming popular by the late nineteenth century, as some collectors saw the value in preserving these spirituals and the old Negro tradition. By the mid-twentieth century, African-American culture via the blues was more heavily integrated into the folk music revival, when music collectors, disillusioned by the overt commercialism and bourgeois materialism which had already corrupted *authenticity* in the folk music scene, looked to the bluesman as a truer embodiment of the authentic folk ethos.[91]

These collectors, in publicizing and marketing the authentic blues with some recordings dating back to the 1920s, set the stage for the later rebel soundtrack of the 1960s. Rock'n'roll began where two roads converged: the rockabilly of Elvis Presley, himself raised in the Mississippi Delta and heavily influenced by black bluesmen; and the British Invasion led by the Rolling Stones, who idolized the Delta bluesmen and just wanted to be "the best blues band in London."[92] As such, white marketing entrepreneurs from Chicago influenced white musicians from the American South and from postwar London, who combined to create a phenomenon that would change the world. All of them stood on the shoulders of disenfranchised black men from the Mississippi Delta. The poetic prose of W.E.B. Du Bois traces the connection between old Negro spirituals and contemporary American musical culture, and argues the songs – not just the blues - of white America have been "distinctively influenced" by the Sorrow Songs and melodies of Negro slaves and their descendents.[93]

An increasing nostalgia for the years before the Great War and before the Great Depression sentimentalized not only the artisan communities of the provincial small town, but also looked for a remedy to the debilitating economic, cultural, and racial ailments currently wreaking havoc on the nation's social fabric. Folk music, then, served not only to codify a sense of authenticity of roots, but also offered a clue to an earlier time, a time which might hold the key to mending the economic, social and political challenges in the present.[94]

The 1930s saw a renewed wave of folk revival during the Great Depression, when the perceived purity and authentic character of folk spoke to Americans battling a devastating national emergency. Many Americans placed hardship and blame at the feet of business and political leaders - and the institution of capitalism - and found courage and strength of national character in ordinary folk. Whereas the Colonial revival was very much a pro-establishment movement, honoring, in the words of John D. Rockefeller, Jr., the lessons of "our forefathers to the common good," the folk revival scene of the 1930s was very much *anti-establishment*, privileging folk and vernacular culture – sometimes radical - over that of the ruling parties of the day.[95]

Our master is a 'patriot' true
Red wealth he has galore,
And all good things that Labor brings,
He's locked up in his store;
But if, like men, you'll organize,
His reign will be no more,
And he will go where he belongs
A shoveling copper ore.

Remember, then, the six hour day
Must be our first demand;
For miners from our ranks each day
From death receive a call;
The miner's 'con' you soon will see
Will lose its deadly pall,
And we'll make this camp a grand old spot
For the workers, one and all

— *"ORGANIZE" BY JAMES FERRITER (1919). AMERICAN FOLK SONG*

By the 1940s, the folk music scene was heavily influenced by leftist politics, with songs that promoted labor unions and racial justice, and sang against economic inequality. As such, the folk revival was not simply about paying homage to the past; the folk singer/songwriter worked within a musical tradition to confront present-day challenges and concerns. However, by the

1950s and under the watch of a much more conservative political leadership, folk music had for the most part ditched its overt leftist political slant. In the early 1960s, New York City's Greenwich Village harbored a folk scene alive and well. "The beats had been brained into existentialism, but the folkniks were full of piss and vinegar and ready to make a lot of noise about change."[96] Greenwich Village had for decades buzzed with an enthusiasm that can only emerge from a rebellious sensibility. Folk and rhythm & blues singer Richie Havens recalls of the early 1960s, "We instinctively knew that big changes in our American culture were brewing all around us. The air was electric and it was going to be like that for most of the decade."[97]

By the late 1960s, however, even Greenwich Village's prince of folkniks, Bob Dylan, was romancing the electric guitar, and folk music's sinking popularity among a growing youth culture gave way to the noisier rebel soundtrack of rock'n'roll. Across the 1950s and '60s, the rise of rock'n'roll shook the aesthetic and moral sensibilities of middle-class adult society.[98] Historian Ronald Cohen looks at the folk music revival and the subsequent triumph of rock'n'roll, and finds that by the mid-century, a backlash against the increasingly rebellious youth culture was growing. The inmates were running the asylum. Youth culture challenged the moral, aesthetic, and racial hierarchies long ago established by their elders, and this challenge was now blasting from rock'n'roll's amplifiers, from the radio dial, and from the hi-fi. "There was considerable alarm."[99]

RADICAL, GUT-WRENCHING CHANGE

Leo Marx concluded *Machine in the Garden* with the prediction that by 1964, its date of publication, the pastoral response to industrialization would begin to fade into an anachronism. When the 1960s and beyond instead saw a renewed devotion to environmentalism and radicalism, Marx later acknowledged "a much deeper ideological continuity" between pastoralism of the nineteenth century and the counterculture movement of the 1960s.[100] Indeed, 1960s radicals were equally repulsed by and reviled the "technocratic direction" of their own contemporary American society.

In 1966, *TIME* magazine named Youth its annual Man of the Year, citing "For better or for worse, the world today is committed to accelerating change: radical, wrenching, erosive of both traditions and old values."[101] The middle class felt itself challenged on several fronts: a youthful and rebellious counterculture; civil rights activists demanding fundamental changes to the nation's social and legal structures; and antiwar protesters attacking not only the elder generation's foreign policy, but its very legitimacy as well. By the 1960s, well over a century of antimodern sensibility in artistic, intellectual, and public spheres spoke to an ongoing alarm regarding the machine's encroachment in the garden and the disruptions of modernity on the human psyche.

Remedies to this alarm manifested in the cultural revivals of Colonial architecture, American folk music, and, as we shall see, the nation's preindustrial maritime history. If the threat of massive change in the prevailing social structure and hegemonic order created a collective sense of nostalgia for a more "authentic" cultural landscape during the Progressive Era, the landscape of challenge and dissent in the 1960s provides a most dynamic matrix in which grew a resurging interest in heritage commemoration and historic preservation.

In New York City, this renewed interested turned to the city's old seaport district, to a different time, to the nation's Golden Age of Sail, as worthy of remembrance and commemoration of a time *when we were good*. The belief that the natural landscape – for Olmsted in the 1860s this meant the parks, for Seaport founder Peter Stanford and the Friends of South Street in the 1960s this meant the sea and the harbor – would positively influence the city dweller's mind and soul and would make for a better citizenry, rotates upon an axis of urban turmoil. While Olmsted was confronting the chaos of increasing immigration and industrialization, Friends of South Street were confronting the chaos of the Civil Rights era, Vietnam War protests, and the "meaningless of the age." Underlying the process of historic preservation during the culturally fracturing Age of Aquarius was the impetus to resuscitate the collective heroism of a potentially fleeting and yet seemingly fundamental American identity.[102]

Chapter 2

BATTLE LINES BEING DRAWN

The world today is asking a terrible question – a question
which every citizen of this Republic should be putting to
himself: what sort of people are we, we Americans? And the
answer which much of the world is bound to return is that
we are today the most frightening people on this planet.[103]

— ARTHUR SCHLESINGER, JR.,
CITY UNIVERSITY OF NEW YORK COMMENCEMENT SPEECH *(1968)*

The country was in a really profound state of
turmoil… The country was coming unhinged.[104]

— *NEH* CHAIRMAN WILLIAM ADAMS *(2014)*

The demolition of New York's grandiose Pennsylvania Station in 1964 was the rallying point that spurred the city's historic preservation movement – practically hibernating since the Progressive Era – to action. New York City's Mayor Robert Wagner signed the Landmarks Preservation Law in response to this publically controversial demolition of McKim, Mead and White's monumental homage to classical architecture and the power of public art and in response to the outrage Penn Station's demolition evoked from historically-minded citizens and arts organizations speckled across the city. Bolstered by its meager ration of power, the Landmarks Preservation Commission had, by 1966, designated a string of the city's Colonial Era structures to the National Historic Landmarks registry, including St. Paul's Chapel, the Morris-Jumel Mansion, the Voorlezer's House, and the Old Merchant's House.

Commemoration of the city's founding fathers, their homes and accomplishments, dominated historic preservation across the 1960s and '70s. Conventional wisdom locates the re-emergence of the preservation impulse as a reaction against the ahistorical nature of modernist urban planning and the historically callous urban renewal bulldozer. Certainly, this reaction against modernist urban planning fueled the impulse to salvage what remained of the eighteenth and nineteenth century cityscape. However, the larger social and political landscape of the 1960s factors significantly into any analysis of historic preservation and heritage commemoration across the decade. Plans for lower Manhattan's South Street Seaport Museum and the Fraunces Tavern museum block both emerged in the 1960s as commemorative sites dedicated to remembering the city's maritime history. As these plans to commemorate the country's maritime prowess as a powerful beacon of American vigor and prosperity emerged mere blocks from one another, the fundamental identity and foundational ideals of American society were being challenged on several vocal and demanding fronts.

Popular magazines *TIME, LIFE, Harper's Weekly, Esquire,* and *The Atlantic Monthly* devoted issue after issue to a new generation of malcontents: counterculture youth, anti-war activists, Black Power activists, student protestors… What exactly did these rebels want? Permeating media coverage of civil rights and student protests, anti-war and counterculture demonstrations, sit-ins, be-ins, takeovers, assassinations, sex, LSD, and battle lines being drawn was a sense of ubiquitous challenge to The Establishment, to the status quo, to what sort of nation America had become. The operating structures of modern American society – capitalism, the military-industrial complex, the consumer's republic, the hierarchy of race - incited protest, violence, and conflict among a younger generating seemingly hell-bent on questioning the very existence of American exceptionalism. Media coverage - ramped up in both timeliness and ubiquity on network nightly news broadcasts, in popular weekly magazines, through photo essays and music criticism – prompted the nation to ask itself, *what sort of people are we, we Americans?*

In the 1960s, *LIFE* magazine was the publication of record of contemporary and popular culture. Millions of Americans – largely white and middle-class - watched Walter Cronkhite's nightly television newscast on CBS, they watched their sons being killed in the jungles of Vietnam and racial tensions flare in cities across the country, and they saw Peter Ut's photos of napalmed children in the pages of *LIFE* magazine, wondering where their country was going. A search through *TIME* and *LIFE* magazines' archives today provides a unique and compelling visual account of contemporary life across the mid-twentieth century. Through its exposes and photo essays, "the magazine sought to influence attitudes and shape perceptions of popular culture" of the day.[105]

In *Once Upon a Distant War,* military historian William Prochnau assures the millennial reader that during the mid-century, publishing mogul Henry Luce's *TIME* and *LIFE* magazines:

> Wielded their power in places that the other great media institutions of the day, the *New York Times*, did not bother to go. The *Times* could take the intelligentsia, and did. But *LIFE* sat on the coffee table of every middle class home in America; The *Times* pitched straight at the ruling elite and became part of it. Henry Luce took middle America.[106]

TIME magazine covered "Protest: The Banners of Dissent," "Hippies: Philosophy of a Subculture," "Speed Kills," "Doctrines of the Dropouts," and "the Politics of Yip;" while its sister publication *LIFE* offered photo essays capturing mayhem on American streets and in the Vietnamese jungle with "The Spectacle of Racial Turbulence in Birmingham," "To L.B.J.: What IS Our Aim in Vietnam?" "Selma: The Savage Season Begins,"

"Arson and Street War: Most Destructive Riot in U.S. History," "Plot to 'Get Whitey!' Negro Revolt: The Flames Spread," "Runaway Kids," and "University Under Siege." *Harper's Weekly* reported, often through long-form journalism than ran well over sixty pages in length, "Anti-Americanism in America," "Rebellious Students and Their Counterrevolution," and "America 1968: The Politics of Violence," while *The Atlantic Monthly* explored the nation's "Sense of Crisis" and "The War Against the Young," tried to make sense of "The Battle of the Pentagon," considered we might in fact be "Misunderstanding Our Student Rebels," and revealed the glaring generation gap with "The Class of '43 is Puzzled." Music of the late '60s was heavily influenced by drugs and sex of the counterculture, daily newspapers and television reporting brought the friction of protest, urban rioting, LSD trips, and the bloody reality of the Vietnam war broadcast into American middle class homes on a daily basis. If challenge, on the whole, came from a minority percentage of the nation's population, its media-generated influence on the public consciousness cannot be underestimated. In the words of writer Alfred Kazin, *everybody felt it.*

> The once-solid core of American life – the cement of loyalty that people tender to institutions, certifying that the current order is going to last and deserves to – this loyalty, in select sectors, was decomposing... The liberal-conservative consensus that had shored up national satisfaction since 1945 – the interwoven belief in economic growth, equality of opportunity, and the Cold War – had fallen afoul of black revolt and Vietnam, and it was as if once the keystone of the arch was loosened, the rest of the structure teetered.[107]

— Todd Gitlin, President, Students
for a Democratic Society (1963)

Determining whether the decade spanning 1960-1970 was, quantitatively or qualitatively, *the most* internally divisive, externally violent, riotous or challenging in American history bears little impact here. Firstly, *the decade* is an arbitrary marker of time, although we tend to reflect on both personal histories and larger collective histories in terms of this classification. We characterize decades as "gay," "roaring," or obsessed with "me." Further, American society has known challenge and dissent from its very foundation. The 1860s, by all accounts, saw a country coming unglued. Our purpose here is not to argue the 1960s was *the* most turbulent decade known to American history. What matters is the *collective perception* of an American public which experienced an increasing and ubiquitous climate of dissent against established leadership, challenge to the postwar consensus of national unity, and disillusionment with the middle-class status quo and its cultural and political hegemony. In real time.

By 1968, sixteen out of seventeen American homes owned a television set, marking a new cultural phenomenon. The sounds of Americans running from billy club wielding cops on our city streets, joined by the sounds of machine gun fire rattling a jungle across the globe, blasted into American homes on a nightly basis. Images of napalm explosions above Vietnamese villages competed with images of African-Americans pinned against shop windows by high-pressure water hoses in Birmingham. The sounds of college students chanting, "Hey, hey, LBJ, how many kids did you kill today?" were answered by the sounds of Buffalo Springfield singing "What a field day for the heat." Any sense of national consensus uniting the country during WWII and during the immediate postwar boom was coming undone in the 1950s and became an intensified national concern by the 1960s. In this landscape, commemoration of a glorified history served to shore up the cultural authority of a perceptively more noble American identity and developed as part of a larger conversation which asked, *what sort of people are we, we Americans?* Eliza Greatroix' 1875 nostalgia for the Colonial Era's seemingly proper observance of class distinctions and the civility that came with a respected – if not coerced – social hierarchy would still be shared by many in 1960, but would face increasing scrutiny and challenge in the years to come.

Street riots, draft card burnings, anti-war demonstrations, a university takeover, and the hippie invasion combined to alter the physical and social landscape of New York City and reflected *The Movement's* local presence. However, in much broader terms, the burgeoning social and political upheaval and dissent – on a national scale – and the increasing and ever-present role of the mass media in providing traction and a sense of ubiquity to this dissent, raised a larger question, not only for New Yorkers, but for the nation as a whole. That question - *what sort of people are we, we Americans?* - would fuel the impulse to commemorate the nation's earlier glory as a beacon of vigor and prosperity at the site of its maritime roots.

THE FIFTIES: THE SILENT GENERATION

We've grown unbelievably prosperous and we
maunder along in a stupor of fat.[108]

— *ERIC GOLDMAN FOR HARPER'S MAGAZINE (JANUARY 1960)*

We know that the 1950s was not so neatly unified or harmonious as popular perception might have described in the decades leading towards the new millennium, nor can we rely on Hollywood productions such as *Happy Days, Laverne and Shirley,* or *American Graffiti* to paint a nuanced picture of the postwar decade for later generations. Constraints by race and gender meant that not everyone – minorities and women included – felt the good life was equally accessible to all. Large numbers of Americans most certainly felt abandoned in the great rush towards prosperity brought on by the boom in the postwar economy and the surge in suburbanization. We can't fit the Fifties into a tidy package of harmony, national consensus, and increasing prosperity, and yet the decade known as harboring the Silent Generation reveals an outward push towards consensus and hegemony that would come under attack a few years later.[109]

Cultural representations of family life in the '50s and for its contemporary audience – television shows like *Leave It To Beaver, The Donna Reed Show,* and *Father Knows Best* – depicted white middle class life as the ideal. Even when the realities of a more diverse American experience said otherwise, the *cultural image* of the American experience was that of the white, middle class, nuclear family.[110] A 1957 report, based on national interviews, found forty percent of young men wanted to be just like their fathers. Father knew best. Young adults of the '50s became known as the Silent Generation, trudging through the Cold War which required Americans to unite against the Soviet enemy; any hint at diverse expressions or ideology could be – and was - charged as subversive, un-American, and treasonous. The 1950s saw millions of Americans "nationalist almost to the point of nativism," characterized by a "self-righteous sense of American superiority [steeped in] pride in democracy, free enterprise, and material success."[111] Looking back on his Harvard Class of '43 from 1968, Nicholas von Hoffman writes in *The Atlantic* of his generation's moral dilemma, a generation accused of striking a "devil's bargain" with its government. That bargain, younger critics were charging, included a lifetime-pass to Full Employment and the Consumer's Republic, complete with proliferating acquisitions and federally-subsidized mortgage payments, in exchange for more than a little apathy and a collective agreement to look the other way while the bomb-builders and the bomb-droppers ramped up anti-Communist aggression across the globe.[112]

For the majority of white Americans, the payoff promised for hard work and respect for the established power structure was a share in the nation's increasing fortunes. This was the social contract. During the economic boom of the postwar years, an expanding middle class was living comfortably amidst a veritable cornucopia, fueled by a thriving industrial economy. However, signs of discontent and disease become measurable when the decade is examined under more careful scrutiny: the number of life insurance policies increase remarkably during this decade, as does the number of Americans seeking psychiatric care. Increases in personal debt, concerns with national security, and a festering Jim Crow reveal a generation not as fat and happy as the next generation would argue.

Indeed, across the 1950s, music and film aimed at a growing postwar youth culture created rebellious teen idols like Marlon Brando in *The Wild One*, James Dean in *Rebel Without a Cause*, Elvis Presley, Lenny Bruce, J.D. Salinger's Holden Caulfield, and the satirical force of *Mad Magazine*. Suddenly, teen angst and rebellion were the new normal, with a generation beginning to move in a very different direction from that of its parents. Buoyed by growing media outlets, teen rebellion increasingly became part of the pop-cultural landscape.[113] While forty percent of young men reported wanting to be just like their fathers, a growing teen culture rejected middle-class norms and challenged the perceived hypocrisy of contemporary life. Young people of the 1950s crossed established racial boundaries when they danced to rhythm & blues, devoured with devilish delight *Mad Magazine's* mockery of mainstream weeklies like *LIFE* and *Reader's Digest*, and read with vigor novels that explored the alienation of youth, most notably embodied in Salinger's protagonist, Holden Caulfield.[114] Confronted with the atrocities of WWII, this generation had witnessed the consequences of passivity and many felt a subsequent skepticism towards authority. By the mid-1960s, magazine articles and books examined why the Fifties, a seemingly prosperous and contented decade, had reared a new generation growing increasingly cynical and delinquent.[115] A vocal faction of the baby boom cohort, raised on skepticism and haunted by the atrocities of WWII, was ready to say good riddance to a decade chastised as "overfed, oversanctified, and overbearing."[116]

THE SIXTIES: RAGE AGAINST THE MACHINE

We are people of this generation, bred in at least modest comfort, housed now in universities, looking uncomfortably to the world we inherit.

— THE PORT HURON STATEMENT OF THE STUDENTS FOR A DEMOCRATIC SOCIETY (JUNE 11, 1962)

While the political and social activism that characterizes the '60s can trace its origins to a much deeper history of American rebellion and resistance, the emerging role of mass media in giving national traction to the rage marks a significant shift in the way American culture was now both reported on and, at the same time, created.[117] *The Movement* of the '60s, as it would be known, began on February 1, 1960 at a Woolworth's in Greensboro, North Carolina when four black students from the North Carolina Agricultural and Technical College sat down at a white-only lunch counter. Belonging to the youth chapter of the local NAACP, the quiet protestors of Jim Crow segregation were refused service but sat all the same, returning the following day with twenty-five additional supporters. By the fifth day of sitting-in, over three hundred protestors joined the original four and the protest attracted national media attention, fueling further sit-ins across the country. Within two months, fifty-four cities in nine states witnessed sit-ins related to the Civil Rights Movement.

The sit-in was not a new form of civil disobedience. National Association for the Advancement of Colored People (NAACP) and Congress of Racial Equality (CORE) activists had sat-in across the South during the 1940s and '50s, protesting ongoing segregation in public accommodations, but these earlier events rarely received national media coverage and were thus relegated to insignificant status. (If no one hears you protest, did a protest occur?) These sit-ins and public protests, as well as those organized in May 1960 against the House Un-American Activities Committee at San Francisco's City Hall, inspired and fueled a burgeoning white student protest movement that took lessons from black civil rights activists.[118] As with the musical trend sweeping from rhythm & blues to rock'n'roll, white middle class children took their lead from black children of the Jim Crow South. *The Movement*, from the very start, was action-oriented and self-determined: we are going to establish a better form of society right here, right now. We are not going to ask for it; we are going to take it.

LIFE magazine, published by Time-Life Incorporated, was one of the most popular weeklies of the decade, enjoying an average weekly circulation of 6,700,000 in 1960. Flip through any issue of *LIFE* in the early 1960s and one finds advertisements dominated by life insurance companies, home appliances, vodka and gin, women's hair color products, American made automobiles, and travel ads to the Bahamas. The weekly's target audience was one that was white and middle-class, enjoying enough disposable income or good credit rating to be able to participate widely in the expanding consumer's republic. In 1960, the magazine's top articles focus on Hollywood stars and starlets, the crisis in the Congo, democracy and the world, the Rockefellers, fashion, modern living, and sports. The magazine's cover photos are as likely to feature models and actresses as world events.

Only a sprinkling of articles in 1960 speaks to domestic trouble, issues of civil rights, or nagging disquiet. A May 23 cover article examines "A Crucial

U.S. Debate on our National Purpose," while a September 19 photo essay reports "The Negroes Drive for Right to Vote, Learn, Practice Politics." Glossy photos depict well-dressed African-Americans lined up outside a courthouse in Haywood County waiting to register to vote. Included is a map depicting various locations of recent sit-ins across the South. The magazine's conveyance of any sense of simmering domestic disquiet is underwhelming in 1960. The reader need not be alarmed.

By 1961, the sit-in as a form of protest against continued segregation of public accommodations in the South was trumped by that summer's series of Freedom Rides. On December 5, 1960 the Supreme Court declared segregated interstate bus terminals unconstitutional and ordered the integration of interstate buses. More frequently than not, southern authorities ignored this ruling. Enter the Congress of Racial Equality (CORE), under the direction of James Farmer, and the Freedom Rides: integrated bus rides into southern cities which meant "to provoke the southern authorities into arresting us and thereby prod the Justice Department into enforcing the law of the land." The subsequent attacks on the Freedom Riders were dramatic, public, and horrifying. Locals set fire to a bus headed to Anniston, Alabama; pipe and chain-wielding Ku Klux Klan members attacked men and women as they disembarked a Birmingham-bound to use the restroom facilities. Among the casualties was a sixty-one year old Freedom Rider who suffered permanent brain damage from his injuries. In Montgomery, Alabama a mob attacked Freedom Riders as their bus pulled in to the station, where women were beaten with clubs and men were left lying unconscious. Eyewitnesses reported policemen stood idly by. One man lay bleeding with spinal cord damage for two hours before authorities were called for transport to the local hospital. Montgomery police commissioner L.B. Sullivan announced that his force had "no intention" of protecting a bunch of out-of-town "troublemakers" intent on bringing disruption to its city.[119] For generations of white southerners, reared in a landscape of racial segregation in which Jim Crow *defined* their very minds and lives, the actions of these civil rights protesters tore through the existing social landscape and thoroughly challenged the attitudes and customs and race-based ideology of many white Americans. For many white southerners, a beloved and treasured way of life was vanishing before their eyes.[120]

Throughout 1963, *LIFE* informs the American public of the lives of the Soviet people; astronauts and the space race; the crisis in Cuba; what high school youth are up to; American troops in Vietnam; and the shocking assassination of President Kennedy. Magazine coverage is increasingly focused on foreign and domestic turmoil, exposing "The Viscous Fighting in Vietnam," in which full color photos depict a napalm strike in the Vietnamese jungle, Vietnamese troops and their captured Vietcong prisoners, and "a field of death" – Vietcong soldiers slain by the dozens, face up and face down in the mud, their captured comrades huddled at the edge of the camera's frame.

The May 17 issue includes a photo essay entitled "They Fight A Fire That Won't Go Out; The spectacle of racial turbulence in Birmingham." Inside, the reader is confronted with full-page photos of African-Americans pinned to storefront windows by high-pressure water hoses wielded by the Birmingham Fire Department, or else splayed out on the sidewalk under the pressure of those hoses. The accompanying text reads, "The pictures on these eleven pages are frightening." Photos capture a violent reaction to a non-violent demonstration, the brutal force used by white firemen against African-American civil rights demonstrators, exposing the deep chasm between white and black in contemporary American society. More photos capture attack dogs biting at the behinds of African-Americans, the dog's teeth snarling and clothing being torn away from bodies.

The domestic brutality here trumps the images of a foreign war: this savagery is happening on our own city streets. Robert Kennedy, brother of the President, Attorney General and future presidential candidate himself, takes keen and sudden interest in the Civil Rights Movement and convinces his brother to do the same. Later in Atlantic City, New Jersey, Mrs. Fannie Lou Hamer testifies in front of the Democratic National Committee as to her arrest following a voter registration workshop, and describes the subsequent beatings she suffered while incarcerated at the Montgomery County Jail. Mrs. Hamer, an African-American voting rights activist and civil rights leader, was placed in a jail cell with two African-American men, who were thereby ordered by State Highway Patrolmen to beat her with a blackjack until the men were "exhausted:"

> All of this on account we want to register, to become first-class citizens, and if the Freedom Democratic Party is not seated now, I question America, is this America, the land of the free and the home of the brave where we have to sleep with our telephones off of the hooks because our lives be threatened daily because we want to live as decent human beings, in America?[121]

... What sort of people are we, we Americans?

RED DIAPER BABIES

Taking a cue from the Civil Rights Movement's practice of civil disobedience, student activists – generally white, wealthy, well educated, and articulate – shifted concerns from black voter registration in the South to the New Left and the Free Speech Movement by 1965. White students who had become involved with the Student Non-Violent Coordinating Committee (SNCC), an organization founded in 1960 intended to support southern civil rights groups through a network of student affiliation and communication, generally believed in the illegitimacy of racial segregation and questioned the moral authority of the reigning Fifties' status quo.[122]

The Students for a Democratic Society (SDS) was founded at the University of Michigan-Ann Arbor and spearheaded by undergraduate Tom Hayden. In 1961 the group met at Port Huron, outside Detroit, with the goal of defining its political and social positions. From this early effort emerged a manifesto, entitled The Port Huron Statement, in which these young academics from rather privileged backgrounds acknowledged their comfortable status in the nation's socio-economic hierarchy and were not pleased with the world upon which they now looked. "We are people of this generation, bred in at least modest comfort, housed now in universities, looking uncomfortably to the world we inherit." The Port Huron Statement rejected the pervasive ideology of the 1950s, echoed in Paul Goodman's *Growing Up Absurd,* in its declaration that individuals – *not* the collective, not the power structure, not the prevailing elite, *i.e.* most certainly *not* the status quo – should direct the political, social, and economic processes that structure American society.[123] The SDS and its political base, the New Left, borrowed strategies such as the sit-in, protest march, and nonviolent demonstration from the Civil Rights Movement. The dynamism of the SDS was located in its declaration that change was imminent, that the younger generation would form the template for revolt, and that *permanent opposition* was the way to avoid the inevitable corruption that power and establishment wrought.[124]

Mario Savio, a student at the epicenter of campus dissent and protest - the University of California Berkeley - was named President of the local Friends of the SNCC after travelling to Mississippi to participate in the Mississippi Freedom Summer's black voter registration drive. In December 1964, Savio led a takeover of UC Berkeley's Sproul Hall on behalf of the newly formed Free Speech Movement, and on the steps of Sproul Hall avowed his generation's responsibility to say *Enough. Stop. This has to stop*:

> There is a time when the operation of the machine becomes so odious, makes you so sick at heart, that you can't take part…and you've got to put your bodies upon the gears… and you've got to make it stop.[125]

What of *the machine* had become so odious? What need to adopt a platform of permanent opposition, and against what forces? Savio and his cohort, born at the tail end of World War II, felt they had grown up in an absurd time in which the responsible citizen was compelled to question authority, to question the very existence of reality, because Nazi atrocities had guaranteed that nothing was beyond the realm of human cruelty. Authority must not be followed idly. Savio's generation had learned that one had an obligation to speak up. Silence was not an excuse. Silence made you culpable. Everything must be questioned.

In December 1964, the College Press Service named 1964 the "Year of Protest on Nation's Campuses." Actually, only a minority of students was ever involved in any campus protest. And yet media attention – from campus publications, to weekly magazines, to nightly news coverage, to national newspapers – presented its audience with a steady stream of student protest and demonstration. Media coverage and the ensuing public dialogue spread the conversation surrounding detractors and dissent. There were, however, conservative student groups actively protesting the protesters. The Young Americans for Freedom counter-protested the demands of the New Left *red diaper babies* – the term applied to the children of American communist activist parents, and left-leaning themselves - and through the YAF's *New Guard* charged that Free Speech advocates were simply cry-babies, demanding rule over the university's quite competent power structure.[126] During his 1964 acceptance speech for the Republican nomination to the presidential election, conservative Barry Goldwater criticized the unruly and amoral culture of dissent which threatened the very fabric of American society, speaking for the deep conservatives who claimed victory at the convention:

> Tonight there is violence in our streets, corruption in our highest offices, aimlessness among our youth, anxiety among our elderly, and there's a virtual despair among the many who look beyond material success toward the inner meaning of their lives. And where examples of morality should be set, the opposite is seen... I seek an America proud of its past, proud of its ways, proud of its dreams and determined actively to proclaim them.[127]

Goldwater's charge that America must be proud of its history and heritage, proud of its culture and proud of its vision, indicates a conservative admonishment against the New Left's rabble-rousing. *Goddammit, this is America! Be proud! Proclaim our strength and our morality and our heritage!* Barry Goldwater was not the only American who felt this way, and his words reflect a considerable portion of society that felt itself under attack from within its own borders. The foundation upon which a tradition of cultural authority rested was being shaken by a minority of malcontents who did not simply disagree with a particular party line or political agenda, but who challenged the very legitimacy of established authority and leadership. A *New York Times* reporter, covering the convention, noted the conservative Right's discontent stemmed from nostalgia and a yearning for a simpler time when "we did not have to worry about overcrowded cities and Negroes demanding their rights and foreign countries refusing to follow the American way." The *Times* reporter notes a pervading sense of frustration, not only related to domestic strife, but to "the state of the world."[128] The very term *nostalgia* ushers in a host of conservative sensibilities, a wishful and melancholy sentiment for a lost – if mythical – past.

ANTI-AMERICANISM IN AMERICA

By the mid-1960s, the various movements challenging multiple facets of American society – including its foreign policy, domestic policy, civil rights, capitalism, higher education, the generational divide, the American Dream, and the ideals and values of modernism – constituted a very real voice of dissent and challenge to the status quo. *The Movement* was primarily a movement of young people, and this was new. From middle-class college students, to hippie dropouts, to political dissenters, the youth of America was, for the first time in history, steering a national course.

The influence of television on *The Movement* and on how the American public perceived this barrage of challenge was tremendous. TV played a pivotal role in alerting the American public to these voices of dissent and offered a public arena for the demands of protestors. By 1960 Americans had purchased over fifty million television sets. Contemporary writers remind us that in our current age of real-time journalism via the Internet and smart phones and twenty-four-hour news coverage, news is disseminated on a minute-by-minute basis to an audience much less unified than that of the 1960s, when millions of Americans *simultaneously* watched the *CBS Evening News with Walter Cronkite* and *The Huntley-Brinkley Report* on NBC. Walter Cronkite's nightly send-off, "That's the way it is," informed millions of Americans en masse of the news of the day, creating a collective and unified experience surrounding the day's events. To offer some perspective: on the day of the attack on Pearl Harbor, there were a mere ten thousand television sets in American homes. During the Tet Offensive twenty-seven years later, ninety-four percent of American homes had a television set. Such a change over a quarter century is among the most profound in American cultural history. Public perception as to the state of the nation and the state of the world, while formed individually, was created contemporaneously and on a scale previously unknown.

With media spreading this "cultural panic" of a rebellious youth culture via the evening news, in published weeklies, through rock'n'roll lyrics, and on television, the events of the decade began to morph into a larger gestalt, an identity crisis, symbolized by well-equipped policemen wielding guns and billy clubs against unarmed civil rights demonstrators; fire hoses and attack dogs bearing down on protestors; tear gas and burning cities from Birmingham to Boston. Images were key in the creation of public culture in the 1960s and no print publication provided more comprehensive visual coverage of the week's events than *LIFE* magazine. The magazine's headlines and photo essays had grown more alarming since the start of the decade, and to a middle class reader, headlines such as "Plot to 'Get Whitey'" indicated a volatile racial situation adding to an already troubling cultural landscape. As Walter Cronkite did through the evening news, *LIFE* magazine did through print media: these media productions helped to create a shared experience in the interpretation of the country's often-staggering cultural climate.

In 1965, the majority of Americans supported President Johnson's policy in Vietnam. Still, questions circulated as to our nation's role in what appeared to be a matter of keeping the communist North Vietnamese out of their weaker neighbor's affairs. *LIFE* editors rolled out the New Year with a direct appeal to the President, published in the opening pages of the January 8 issue, asking, "What IS Our Aim in Vietnam?" Racial antagonisms and student discord at home remain the weightiest issues on the home front, with a February 26 article exposing the "Plot to Behead the Statue of Liberty," in which an undercover rookie cop uncovers a plot by the Black Liberation Front to blow the head and arms off of the Statue of Liberty, and to blow up the Liberty Bell and the Washington Monument. The acts of terrorism were meant to show the BLF's hatred for its native country. In a conversation with the undercover cop, one of the ringleaders referred to Lady Liberty as "that damned old bitch."[129]

A few weeks later, the March 19 cover headline reads "Civil rights face-off at Selma: The Savage Season Begins" over a photo of African-American civil rights marchers crossing a bridge into Selma to awaiting Alabama State Troopers. The inside photo essay provides eight glossy pages of Alabama troopers swarming upon and tackling African-American marchers to the ground. Readers view full-color photos capturing the state officers spraying tear gas and wielding billy clubs. A caption describes the skirmish, noting the troopers were cheered-on by white onlookers; "Dazed and wounded Negroes helplessly await aid." A following story reports, "U.S. Embassies Are Under Siege," with American embassies in Sudan, Bolivia, Bulgaria, Cairo, Prague, Jakarta, Hue, Uruguay, Budapest, Uganda, Caracas, and Moscow under attack by foreign dissidents. Trouble strikes from within and without and from both directions; America's historically brave and bold image of itself is reduced to glaring inconsistencies and moral ambiguity.

By mid-decade, *LIFE's* pages contain photo essays covering all aspects of the nation's crisis of character, from ongoing urban and racial violence in "Arson and Street War – Most Destructive Riot in the U.S," "Plot to 'Get Whitey,' Red-hot young Negroes plan a ghetto war," and "Negro Revolt: The Flames Spread;" to the escalation in troops in Vietnam and the death of the American Dream in "The Blunt Reality of War in Vietnam" and "Students in a Ferment Chew Out the Nation." In April 1964, students demonstrate by the tens of thousands on the Washington Mall, calling for the U.S. to withdraw its troops from the increasingly controversial Vietnam War. One Stanford University student tells LIFE magazine that he does not believe in the American Dream, while a student from Tufts University adds that *action,* not apathy, is what's needed: "My generation knows we have to strike at the system to make it respond."[130] These students, and tens of thousands like them across the country, were protesting the nation's growing – and increasingly indiscernible – mission in Vietnam. The November 26 *LIFE* cover story, "The Blunt Reality of War in Vietnam," offers twenty-four pages of war coverage. These photos capture Vietnamese mothers carrying their naked and wounded children, tiny casualties resulting from a U.S. jet strafing before landing. One anguished mother's mouth is open in a mid-cry of grief and terror. The reader learns that although Marine medics airlifted the baby to a hospital ship, the child could not be saved.

Antiwar demonstrations deepened into more subversive action in 1965 with the arrival of public draft-card burnings. President Johnson steadily increased the draft in 1965 after ordering the escalation of U.S. forces in Vietnam; draft calls doubled by the end of the year. *LIFE* reported "a rash of draft-card burnings;" *Newsweek* scolded, "No government can condone this kind of defiance and still govern." The *New York Times* reported thousands of young men were trying to escape their patriotic duty by burning draft-cards or by refusing to register or by feigning homosexuality. For those American boys under the age of majority who were given a 1-A status, the option to either take up arms or dodge the draft was made even more problematic in light of the fact these lads had neither the right to vote in or out of office their Commander in Chief. The voting age held steady at twenty-one.

Paul Potter, new President of the SDS, spoke to 25,000 student demonstrators at the April 1965 rally in front of the Washington Monument. If Middle America didn't understand why these New-Left-Free-Speech-Antiwar-Antiestablishment-Youth would forego their patriotic duty and fight with their country the way hundreds of thousands of young American men had done for generations, if the Conservative Right didn't understand, if the Generation Over Thirty didn't understand, then Potter's speech to America, blasted across the pages of *LIFE* magazine and delivered to the front doors of middle-class American homes, reported on by Walter Cronkite - "the voice of God on TV" - on the *CBS Evening News* into millions of American living rooms, would inform the country and the world what, exactly, was wrong with this picture:

The incredible war in Vietnam has provided the razor, the terrifying sharp cutting edge that has finally severed the last vestige of illusion that morality and democracy are the guiding principles of American foreign policy...The further we explore the reality of what this country is doing and planning in Vietnam, the more we are driven toward the conclusion of Senator Morse that the United States may well be the greatest threat to peace in the world today. That is a terrible and bitter insight for people who grew up as we did.[131]

Potter charged that America's moral high-ground bubble had burst. While black Americans struggled for liberty and equality in their own country, the United States government claimed its presence in Vietnam was meant to secure the rights of liberty and equality for the citizens of that far and away nation. The hypocrisy! The SNCC, vocal in antiwar efforts alongside the SDS, released its position paper on Vietnam in the spring of 1966, claiming violence was being perpetrated by the U.S. government against its own citizens. The SNCC was ripping the mask of hypocrisy from the face of national policy.[132]

What sort of people are we, we Americans, when State Troopers club to the ground nonviolent protestors, impervious – no possibility they were unaware - to the reporter's camera and pen? What sort of people are we, we Americans, when ten thousand black Americans take to the streets "in marauding bands," looting, shooting at law enforcement officers, setting fire and causing forty million dollars in property damage in six days in Watts, Los Angeles? What sort of people are we, we Americans, when National Guardsmen are called in to patrol our urban streets with bayonettes? What sort of people are we, we Americans, when foreign *civilians* – women and children and babies and the elderly – are attacked from the sky by napalm strikes delivered by U.S. troops?

FOR WHAT IT'S WORTH[133]
In its 1967 hit "For What It's Worth," rock band Buffalo Springfield sings Steven Still's lyrics of armed men in the streets, vocal youth rebelling against the established hierarchy of their elders, battle lines drawn between young and old, right and left, black and white. Resistance; how many people in the street.[134] Todd Gitlin, former President of the SDS, later described the years 1967-1970 as "a cyclone in a wind tunnel."[135] While *The Movement* always represented a minority of the American population, it was very vocal and

its protest and demonstrations were captured nightly on the evening news and throughout mainstream print media. Voices of *The Movement* attacked just about every institution in American society, from business to religion to government to the armed forces to the consumer's republic. Because the long-held notion of American exceptionalism was predicated upon the conviction – no, the knowledge! – that the American experience was especially unique, founded upon a birthright of Manifest Destiny and ordained by the grace of God, the very structure of the American Way claimed supreme legitimacy across all aspects of the political, economic, and cultural landscape. When the rationales for these institutions came under attack in the 1960s, skepticism, defiance, and rebellion threatened to unhinge the entire system.[136]

LIFE's June 10, 1966 cover image of a disheveled Elizabeth Taylor, playing Martha to husband Richard Burton's George in *Who's Afraid of Virginia Wolfe?* is trumped by the cover's headline, "Plot to 'Get Whitey,' Red-hot young Negroes plan a ghetto war." The editor's note inside the cover pages warns of "a story of hatred and massive, planned violence that few people except the police and the extremists themselves know."[137] The author warns his reader that across the country, a growing cult of Black Power extremists is organizing in the black ghettos. The era of Martin Luther King Jr.'s peaceful resistance is over; chaos and urban rioting are imminent. Earlier in 1966, Stokely Carmichael, elected president of the SNCC, claimed "Black Power!" as the organization's rallying cry and summarily excluded all whites from the SNCC. In a written statement, Carmichael acknowledged that whites had indeed played a critical role in the early successes of the organization, but the time had come for blacks to assume total responsibility for the movement: Black self-determination. Carmichael explained, "We cannot be expected any longer to march and have our heads broken in order to say to whites, come on, you're nice guys. For you are not nice guys. We have found you out."[138] Concerns over an increasing disregard for law and order and heightening racial turmoil reached the highest offices across the country, with future President Richard Nixon cautioning, "Private conversations and public concern are increasingly focusing upon the issues of disrespect for the law and race turmoil."[139] Carmichael's cry for Black Power! was a far cry from the

Civil Right Movement's anthem, Pete Seeger's "We Shall Overcome," just a few short years before.

Indeed, the long hot summers of '67 and '68 became known as "riot season." The August 4, 1967 cover of *LIFE* depicts U.S. armed troops patrolling a Detroit street alight in flames. The magazine's editorial opens with the sound of alarm, describing the current national climate as "cruelly strained," indeed the worst national crisis since Appomattox. Across Omaha, Chicago, Boston, Tampa, Cincinnati, Atlanta, Kansas City, Buffalo, Minneapolis, Plainfield, Newark, and Detroit, "riot season" threatened to rip apart the fabric of the nation.[140]

Washington D.C. Riot, April 1968. Aftermath. Courtesy Library of Congress, Prints & Photographs Online Catalog. No known restrictions on publication.

LIFE's editorial further cautions its reader to the very real possibility of a white backlash against this Negro Revolt; blacks would be unable to defend themselves against a white majority which feels the authorities are unable to keep the peace. This editorial stance is rather shocking in its implicit understanding and potential justification for white vigilantism in the face of black urban revolt. *TIME* magazine reports that in 1967, racial upheavals across 168 cities resulted in 82 deaths, 3,400 injuries, and 18,800 arrests. During the singular month of April, 1968, 202 racial upheavals in 172 cities resulted in 43 deaths, 3,500 injuries, and 27,000 arrests. One month. The summer of 1968 proved less destructive than the previous four summers, however. This, by comparison, was tranquil.[141]

It is important to note that while present-day discussion surrounding this era of urban violence alternates between the terms "riot," "rebellion," or "revolt," in the years between 1964 and 1968 - when the country was in the midst of heat and wrath raining down across urban America - the violence was most certainly characterized as *riotous* in the mainstream press. Mainstream media referred to the summer months of 1967 and 1968 as "riot season." *TIME* and *LIFE* served as a check on the pulse of the nation; these uprisings were most certainly understood as riots to the majority of the country as they were happening. As a journalist for *The Atlantic Monthly* remarked in 1968, *TIME* magazine was "an invaluable publication for revealing what is socially and politically acceptable in the society at any given time."[142] What was socially and politically acknowledged was this charge that the urban crisis had reached a violent and riotous crescendo.

These were violent years for the nation as a whole, and for New York City in particular. New York City firefighters called these *the war years,* owing to the escalation of arson and false alarms. Murders, rapes, and armed robberies skyrocketed in New York City from the late 1960s and into the early 1970s: murders increased from 734 in 1966 to 1,740 in 1973; rapes from 1,154 to 3,735; robberies from 25,539 to 72,750.[143]

1967 arrived with a new challenge to the status quo: hippies and their counterculture. *TIME* was so fascinated with this new breed of rebellious youth - as if chronicling a foreign culture - the editors created an ongoing series: *Hippies.* In 1967, *TIME* covers the counterculture movement with its reporting on "Hippies: Philosophy of a Subculture," "Hippies: Within the Tribe," "Hippies: Dream Farm," "Hippies: Where Have All the Flowers Gone?" "Speed Kills," and "Runaway Kids." The magazine informs its readers of hippie philosophy and cultural practices, including the ideals of utopianism and transcendentalism, the practice of hippie love and "free love," the attraction and dangers of LSD, marijuana, and communal living in crash pads. *TIME* reports hippies are predominantly white, middle class, educated youth, ranging in age from seventeen to twenty-five.

What made this generation so captivating, confusing, and infuriating to its elders was the counterculture dropout mentality, the idea that one could simply opt-out of work, status, money and power: the complete rejection of the American Dream. *TIME* covers hippie weddings and hippie pot farms, bad LSD trips, the gang rape of hippie women, and the recent rash of middle class kids running away to Haight-Ashbury in San Francisco or the East Village in New York City to hook up with fellow hippies in flop houses. Of the tens of thousands of runaway middle class and affluent kids from middle American suburbs, now high on LSD, meth and pot, *TIME* warns: *these could be your kids.* Young girls, fleeing the constraints of their repressive middle-class homes, could "easily" find acceptance and refuge in the flowering hippie subculture. Mothers are photographed searching the city street for their runaway teens.[144]

Tom Wolfe, the American writer whom historian David Farber calls "one of the most perceptive contemporary cultural critics in the Sixties,"[145] travelled with uber-hippie Ken Kesey, author of *One Flew Over the Cuckoo's Nest*, and The Merry Pranksters on a cross-country acid trip in 1964-65. In his subsequent romp, *The Electric Kool-Aid Acid Test,* Wolfe interprets the hippie mindset for anyone amused enough by his New Journalism commentary to enjoy the ride. Wolfe explains to his reader the mindset of the hippie youth, in which the American Dream, and everything mom, dad, grandma and grandpa worked for and fought for and believed in, was pure fantasy:

It was a fantasy world already, this electro-pastel world of Mom&Dad&Buddy&Sis in the suburbs… *you're already there, in Fantasyland,* so why not move off your snug-harbor quilty-bed dead center and cut loose – go ahead and say it – Shazam![146]

Explained through Wolfe's supercharged prose, the hippie mindset and its counterculture philosophy detect very clearly, in all manner of psychedelica and *shazam,* the American Dream was nothing more than fantasy. None of it was real; how did dropping acid make the unreal any *less* real? These hippie kids, far from being disenfranchised, were in fact Superkids! Reared smack-dab in the middle of the nation's cornucopia of wealth and glory: the consumer's republic! Children of the middle-class rejecting the hand that feeds them, challenging The Establishment *from the inside,* abandoning the established structures of American society, clashing with both the elder generation's traditional ideals and the truly disenfranchised urban communities among whom they now "crashed." These hippie kids could *afford* to tune in and drop out. These kids had means, they had status; they had *options.*

It was one thing to upset, disappoint, or terrify one's own family, to run off and join the other delinquents in Tompkins Square Park or the Sunset Strip. It was quite another thing to interrupt the well-oiled machine of capitalism and the free exchange of commodities. On August 24, 1967, hippie-turned-Yippie! and anti-establishment prankster Abbie Hoffman led a group of Yippies! - the cheekily and hastily dubbed Youth International Party - to the floor of the New York Stock Exchange, whereby the dissidents dropped dollar bills over the floor of the nation's leading stock exchange, halting the ticker as brokers scrambled to pick up the discarded George Washingtons. Hoffman then set to burning money in front of aghast, or amused, reporters. This spectacle was an effort to protest capitalism's stranglehold on American society.

Earlier that same year, South Street Seaport Museum founder Peter Stanford – a member of the nation's media circle himself as copy writer for Madison Avenue's Compton Advertising - created an ad celebrating the Stock Exchange's 175th anniversary. The New York Stock Exchange: veritable symbol of capitalism and American economic supremacy. Stanford's ad featured an old print of lower Manhattan's commercial district, including a ship in the background with sails unfurled. While Stanford's advertising copy would bring some nuance to the fabled origin story of Wall Street's great traders of finance, Hoffman's Yippies! were intent on challenging that capitalistic structure altogether.

The following May, Hoffman and his Yippies! held a vernal equinox cel-ebration at New York's Grand Central Station, in which some reported six thousand supporters came out to engage in the "festivities." Someone set off a series of cherry bombs, a melee ensued, and cops charged the crowd, clubbing Yippies! and non-Yippies alike, while the crowd chanted "Seig Heil!" Hoffman was clubbed unconscious. With full media coverage on the scene, the New York City press later termed the event a "police riot." Hoffman's antics with his Yippie! cohort were fueled by spectacle and the power of public display. The Yippie! agenda was to create a spectacle which required media response. It was all part of a grand theater, during which the Yippies! challenged the very basis of capitalism, mass commercialism, authority, and the corporate structure of American society.

Across 1965, '66, and '67, student demonstrators protested the lending practices of Chase Manhattan Bank, headquartered in lower Manhattan. Early in 1965, at the invitation of Standard Bank's chairman, Chase had assumed a minority participation in Standard Bank's South African hold-ings. Through the purchase of what amounted to 14.5% of Standard's shares, Chase now held branches in Johannesburg, South Africa; Lagos, Nigeria; and Monrovia, Liberia. The acquisition of South African branches fueled an uproar among Civil Rights activists in this country, who were seeking ra-cial equality at home and abroad. In March 1965, four hundred demonstra-tors picketed outside Chase Manhattan Bank headquarters at 1 Chase Plaza, across from Battery Park. The predominantly white student protestors decried Chase loans to the white supremacist government of South Africa, shouting "Chase Manhattan supports South African racism!" Protestors from the SDS, CORE, the National Student Christian Federation, and Student Non-Violent Coordinating Committee called for the bank's executives to halt all financial support to South Africa's regime of apartheid. In an era of violent confronta-tion for Civil Rights on American soil, what were the ethical implications of an American institution supporting a racist regime overseas?

In December 1966, protestors again gathered outside of Chase's down-town headquarters, during which time a Chase spokesman indicated the bank had no intentions of pulling its loans out of South Africa. The following

March, Chase's Chairman, David Rockefeller, defended his institution's financial positions at the annual stockholder's meeting. Far from endorsing South Africa's segregationist policies, Rockefeller hoped the Bank's financial dealings would "exert a constructive influence on racial conditions in South Africa."[147] In his *Memoirs*, David Rockefeller recalls:

> The consensus that had unified the country in the postwar period had ended abruptly in the mid-1960s. Strong popular opposition to the Vietnam War and rising unrest in our cities were accompanied by a growing antipathy toward business in general and big banks in particular... I believed Chase did have a responsibility to help redress the legitimate social and economic problems that confronted the country.[148]

Noting the "complex urban issues of the day," Rockefeller felt the communication gap between the generations and between the races "cried out for immediate action." Rockefeller, reared in a climate of inter-generational family philanthropy and currently supporting the Fraunces Tavern museum block project just steps away from Chase headquarters, firmly believed that social responsibility was the obligation of the private sector. The "major ills of our country" required immediate attention, and in his memoirs Rockefeller recounts his eagerness to address the climate of urban unrest. In doing so, he sought to forge a "new image" for Chase Manhattan Bank, which involved charitable giving, personal participation, and a strong philanthropic ideology.[149]

Runaway hippie teenagers invading Tompkins Square Park on New York City's lower east side; subversive Yippies! dropping dollar bills on the floor of the New York Stock Exchange in the city's downtown financial district; young men burning draft cards at the Whitehall Street induction center in lower Manhattan; and protests outside of Chase Manhattan Bank's headquarters are but a few examples of where the decade's era of discord and dissent played out on the streets of New York City. An anti-war rally from Central Park to the United Nations building in April 1967 included hippies as well as Columbia scholars, a prelude, perhaps, to the rash of student takeovers that would spread across university campuses over the next year. In New York City, students at Columbia effectively shut down the University during an occupation that highlighted the social and political divide between student protestors and the status quo.

On April 23, 1968, less than three weeks following the assassination of Dr. Martin Luther King, Jr., 300 chanting students marched into Hamilton Hall and took Dean Henry Coleman hostage. Organized by Columbia University's SDS chapter president, Mark Rudd, the focus of the opposition was two-fold: opposition to the University's plans to build a gymnasium in a nearby public park in Morningside Heights, which would encroach upon the predominantly African-American community that currently used the park; and opposition to CIA and Department of Defense funding to the University for weapons research. Columbia students were joined in their takeover by the Harlem chapter of CORE, the Harlem Committee for Self-Defense, the United Black Front, and the New York chapter of the Student Nonviolent Coordinating Committee. A conservative counter-demonstration group of about 150 students, Students for a Free Campus, protested against the protestors.

With Dean Coleman barricaded in his office, the protestors drafted a mandate, which demanded the University halt all construction plans for the Morningside Park gym; grant amnesty to all students currently facing disciplinary actions for previous demonstrations; remove the ban on campus demonstrations; and proceed with open hearings in any/all future charges against students accused of wrongfully demonstrating. By Day 2 of the takeover, protestors occupied two more campus buildings and the black contingency asked the white protestors to vacate Hamilton Hall and seize an alternate building. White students of the SDS then took over the office of University President Grayson Kirk, while Dean Coleman was released from his captivity at Hamilton Hall. By Day 3 of the takeover, 600 students occupied buildings across the campus, including Low Library. Anti-protest students erected a human blockade and vowed to prevent food and medical supplies from getting inside to the student occupiers. At 2:30 a.m. on April 30, one week after the takeover and at the request of University administration, 1,000 policemen rolled in to remove protestors from the occupied buildings. Geared up for potential confrontation, city police "fanned through the darkened campus" and strategically infiltrated designated "target areas." During negotiations with

CORE, the Harlem Committee for Self-Defense, the United Black Front, and the New York chapter of the Student Nonviolent Coordinating Committee, University administrators agreed at this point to halt plans for the gymnasium construction in Morningside Park.[150]

Painting a picture of this vast ideological divide between a dissatisfied youth culture on the one hand, and the established status quo on the other, Mark Rudd of the SDS and President Grayson Kirk of Columbia University each held fast to his personal conviction that this rift was much larger than one simply between two individuals. When Kirk issued his public statement on April 12, 1968, admittedly disturbed by the "inchoate nihilism" swelling amongst the younger generation, Rudd responded with his own open letter, assuring his elder this ideological conflict was far from over:

> *Our young people, in disturbing numbers, appear to reject all forms of authority from whatever source derived and they have taken refuge in the turbulent and inchoate nihilism whose sole objectives are destructive. I know of no time in our history when the gap between generations has been wider or more potentially dangerous.*
>
> — *GRAYSON KIRK* [151]

> *Dear Grayson, I see it as a real conflict between those who run things now – you, Grayson Kirk – and those who feel oppressed by and disgusted with the society you rule – we, the young people. We can point, in short, to our meaningless studies, our identity crisis, and our repulsion with being cogs in your corporate machines as a product of and reaction to a basically sick society… We will take control of your world, your corporation, your university, and attempt to mold a world in which we and other people can live as human beings.*
>
> — *MARK RUDD* [152]

While the incidences at Columbia University, Grand Central Station, the New York Stock Exchange, and Chase Manhattan Bank involved a relatively small percentage of counterculture activists, Yippie! guru Abbie Hoffman acknowledged the great power of the media in escalating not only these actions, but the ideological torrent underscoring them. One only had to *act* as if the entire youth generation was engaged in the counterculture movement for the myth to become real. The media was critical in hyping and perpetuating this myth, which required amplification in order to create the impression that the State had lost control, had lost its legitimacy to govern.

In light of ongoing events, this impression might not have been much of a stretch for the myriad dissenters now organizing demonstrations across the country. Antiwar protestors *did* argue the State had lost legitimacy with its claim of securing the rights of freedom and equality for citizens of a foreign land, while America's own citizens did not always enjoy these rights at home and were instead clubbed and sprayed under high-pressure hoses; Black Power supporters *did* argue the State had lost legitimacy with its refusal to fully enfranchise the black American community; the New Left and the SDS *did* argue the State had lost its legitimacy to govern due to the "unrepresentative character of the political system [and] its repressive response to human need and protest."[153] The events surrounding the 1968 Democratic National Convention in Chicago were perhaps the pivotal moment highlighting these charges that an illegitimate leadership was coercing its people.

THE AGONY AND THE ECSTASY[154]

> *This new generation of the Left hated the authority*
> *because the authority lied. It lied through the teeth*
> *of corporation executives and Cabinet officials and*
> *police enforcement officers and newspaper editors and*
> *advertising agencies, and in its mass magazines.*[155]
>
> — *Norman Mailer for Harper's Weekly (1968)*

By 1968, Norman Mailer writes the difference between the New Left and the Yippies! was purely insignificant, each group had so influenced the other through demonstration tactics, street activity, and the politics of confrontation. The liberal-conservative consensus that had carried the nation through the postwar years had clearly unraveled, and in 1968 - a year of presidential primaries - that divide was surly felt among the candidates, the delegates, and the general population. When the Republican National Convention convened in Miami in early August, nominee Richard Nixon spoke in defense of good, strong, hardworking Americans everywhere, reminding the nation and the world that the majority of Americans were not shouting in the streets, were not challenging the very foundation of American society, were not maligning the spirit and pride of this great nation. Nixon spoke in the voice of those who insisted that America was in fact good, and could be better still, if we would only get back to the business of progress and the support of private enterprise:

> The voice of the great majority of Americans, the forgotten Americans – the non-shouters; the non-demonstrators. They are not racists or sick; they're not guilty of the crime that plagues the land; they are Black, they are white, they ran businesses and worked blue-collar jobs in factories, they worked in government and served our country on the battlefields of war. They give drive to the spirit of America...lift to the American dream...steel to the backbone of America...good people...decent people...America is a great nation today not because of what government did for people, but because of what people did for themselves over one hundred and ninety years in this country...What we need are not more millions on welfare rolls but more millions on payrolls...The greatest engine of progress ever developed in the history of man: American private enterprise.[156]

Richard Nixon - he of the Checkers Speech, the ultimate straight-arrow upper-class white American, the very embodiment of The Establishment, his wife smiling proudly in her Republican cloth coat - called to private enterprise, to the spirit of hard work and steel and ingenuity, celebrating America as a nation of industry and progress. Nixon implicitly recalls an American origin myth and challenges his supporters to return to those origins. Build the American Dream! Participate in the engine of progress! America was built on the strength and wits of men like you, men of mark, men of brains and brawn! America achieved success because of what people did for themselves for over one hundred and ninety years in this country. Private enterprise: *this* is our heritage, this is our success story! How can we get ourselves, our nation, *back to the garden?*[157] Hippies weren't the only group of Americans looking for a way back to Eden. To Richard Nixon and his conservative supporters, the garden was made up of good people who worked hard, supported private enterprise, and served their country.

Two weeks following the Republican National Convention in Miami, the Democrats convened in the hot summer of Chicago, where the media showed greater concern for what was happening outside the walls of the convention center than within. Congregating in Lincoln Park, thousands of hippies, Yippies!, supporters of the SDS, the Mobe, the Black Panthers, and myriad "freelance militants" gathered in more and in less unified fashion to protest the convention's proceedings. The protest was a general voice of dissent against the candidacy of Vice President Hubert Humphrey – an HH nomination would mean four more years of LBJ's pro-Vietnam War policy – and against the coercive force now routinely being used by local officials against demonstrators.

On behalf of the Yippies!, Hoffman and Rubin had attempted to obtain a permit for the week's festivities, which would include a music festival, various hippie-inspired workshops, and a march across town to make the Democratic conventioneers sit up and listen. Mayor Daley refused to grant such a permit and tensions between the protestors in Lincoln Park and the city ran high. Anticipating a raucous week of confrontation, writers William Burroughs, Norman Mailer, Jean Genet, Mike Royko, and countless journalists writing for *Esquire, Harper's Magazine,* the *Chicago Sun-Times, Newsweek,* the *Washington Post,* the *Chicago American* were on the scene to witness and to record the anticipated spectacle.

In a police raid on the night of August 26 against a gathering of protesters in nearby Lincoln Park, in which "the attack by the police had been ferocious," seventeen reporters were counted among the wounded, including a photographer for the *Washington Post*, two reporters for the *Chicago American*, a photographer and a reporter from *LIFE*, three network television cameramen, and three reporters plus one photographer from *Newsweek*.[158] Todd Gitlin was in Chicago to participate in the demonstrations and described the police riot in which National Guardsmen proceeded "in full battle dress" down Michigan Avenue to join up with an eagerly awaiting Chicago police force, ready for action. Gitlin recalls his wonder, fright, and then elation as the months – no, the years! – of a growing civil discontent rose to a frightening crescendo, and who knew what, exactly, would emerge from the melée that could only ensue. Battle lines were most certainly drawn, confrontation was readily apparent. And while no one could honestly know if he was witnessing a revolution or a counterrevolution – who would be the victor? – that distinction was besides the point. For Gitlin, satisfaction came from knowing that no one could sweep this conflict under the rug. Television cameras were everywhere. Gitlin knew, the crowd knew: The whole world is watching. They can only rule by force. Everyone is going to see.[159]

On Wednesday, after ten thousand demonstrators gathered in Grant Park for a protest rally, someone lowered the American flag and replaced it with a red Communist flag. A fracas ensued. As the police moved in and formed a wedge, Gitlin describes:

> A network television camera recorded a Guardsman in extraterrestrial-looking gas mask halting one driver, telling her to turn around, getting enraged by her hesitation, then poking a grenade launcher in her child's face. And then the Guard in their masks sprayed vast clouds of tear gas from converted flamethrowers slung on their backs, the gas filling the park in every direction and wafting across Michigan Avenue to the Hilton, where eventually it disturbed Hubert Humphrey in his shower.[160]

What sort of people are we, we Americans?...
...The answer is that we are today the most frightening people on this planet.

This was not the Soviet Union, this was not Czechoslovakia, or France, or Italy, or Poland, or Cuba, or any of the countless "other" nations that had witnessed their own series of riotous confrontations between civilians and the militia. This was the United States of America, and this was a nation divided. Divided between black and white, between left and right, between hawk and dove, between old and young, between straights and freaks. Both the nation's and the city's collective identity – whether ever fully realized or not - were in tatters; this was an age of cultural fracturing. This spectacle, this culmination of a near decade of dissent in the long hot summer of 1968, was unacceptable to young hippies and elder statesmen, to Anglos and Black Panthers alike. With Presidential candidate Richard Nixon's campaign slogan in 1968 demanding "Bring Us Together!" many Americans, as had occurred in earlier ages of chaos and concern, looked back in order to go forward.

The proliferating demands of student protesters, antiwar dissenters, counterculture drop-outs, and Civil Rights defenders affected a cross-section of New Yorkers in much the same way they affected a cross-section of Americans across the country: shocked or indifferent, indignant or mystified, consensus is hard to find. Political conservatives, those aligned with Barry Goldwater in 1964 or Richard Nixon in 1968, dug in their heals and called for a return to hard work and gritty determination in order to build the nation onward and upward. These conservatives called for "good, decent people," to shape American enterprise and build upon two hundred years of ingenuity and determination. College students at the City's top university, feeling "oppressed and disgusted" with a society their elders lay before them, demanded a changing-of-the-guard and a more humane world order. The Black Power faction of Harlem lay claim to its turf; Bob Dylan, Joan Baez and their folksie followers in Greenwich Village embodied youthful sexuality and the ideals of democratic freedom; middle-class white New Yorkers listened to *the voice of God on TV,* Walter Cronkite, in attempts to understand and digest the new American drama. The question, *what sort of people are we, we Americans?* begged to be answered. At the core of that fundamental query lies an acute dilemma: *is* there an American identity to be had? And if so, where might we find it?

Chapter 3

PAST PERFECT; HISTORY AND IDENTITY ON THE WATERFRONT

We must now explore how history, memory, and identity converged in ways that made the New York waterfront an iconic, mediated symbol over time. In the summer of 1968, while Republican National Convention delegates were nominating Richard Nixon for the Presidential ticket and reporters were covering nightly police riots against civilian protesters at the Democratic National Convention, while President Johnson continued the nation's escalation of troops in Vietnam, while runaway hippies flooded into the Haight-Asbury in San Francisco and Tompkins Square Park in New York City - some high on LSD or pot, others pregnant, almost all fleeing middle-class homes and the modern conveniences their affluent parents had provided them, while America's moral authority and national character were being challenged both on the streets and through the media, a decidedly better version of collective identity was experiencing a determined resuscitation at New York City's old seaport. *The Movement* of the '60s, in all its forms – from Civil Rights protests, to anti-war protests, to Black Power demands, to student takeovers of their too-conservative universities, to counterculture drop-outs – proved a vocal and often violent challenge to business-as-usual and the reigning political, social, and cultural ideologies upon which the nation had grown. Comprising a similar social-cultural mechanism we find in the commemorative movements of architecture and folk music revival, historic preservation of the city's preindustrial past swelled in the 1960s within this troubling cultural landscape. In New York City, the history and imagery of the city's Golden Age of Sail glowed like a beacon in the midst of a grittier reality.

The realities of a turbulence with which Americans and New Yorkers coped with varying degrees of unease necessitated the creation of public memories. Such memories serve a critical role in the remembrance and renegotiation of America's past in light of the social and political landscape of the present. The physical manifestations of historic memory – whether these take the form of historic preservation of architecture, the creation of public monuments and commemorative sites, or the popularization of old folk tunes – legitimize certain histories and effectively erase others. On the one hand, these representations of history and identity anchor collective memories in the cultural landscape and are especially useful during times of challenge and turmoil; on the other hand, what is left out of the commemorative structure represents a negative space in which certain memories are disregarded or erased as counter to the official narrative. In the search for a usable past at New York City's seaport, which memories might be salvaged at the bottom of the harbor and among the narrow streets and sloped roof buildings? More significantly, which stories did not qualify for remembering, which would not enter the canon of collective memory? Woven into the very pungent sense of place at the mid-century seaport are memories glorious and gritty, dignified and derelict. Boosters of historic preservation at South Street and across lower Manhattan, dissatisfied with what the area had become, sought to remember a better version of the city's seafaring past – and collective spirit – which no longer dominated the cultural landscape of the city's waterfront.

By the mid-twentieth century, the cobbled streets and aging slips of New York's South Street seaport embodied a deeply felt sense of place, where a cultural landscape littered with storehouses of memory still inhabited the district surrounding the aging Fulton Fish Market. Unfortunately, this urban landscape represented the wrong sense of place for both commercial developers and boosters of historic preservation and heritage commemoration projects along the waterfront. By the 1960s, the seaport was gritty and the bustling days of New York as a vibrant port city had quite obviously deteriorated. What remained on the east side of lower Manhattan just south of the Brooklyn Bridge was, by some accounts, a no-man's-land, a dark urban jungle, a jumbled mix of junk shops, narrowly twisted streets, impossible traffic, and the rank stench of the fish stalls comprising one of the last reminders of the city's preindustrial marketplace. At mid-century, the best one could hope for along Fulton Street and Schermerhorn Row was a tasty bowl of chowder or a plate of finnan haddie. Surrounding the cobbled slips of the old seaport, Wall Street's ever-multiplying pillars of finance emerged from the razed nineteenth century landscape in a process of urban renewal.

John De Pol, one of the most prominent engravers of the twentieth century and whose work would feature prominently at the future South Street Seaport Museum, presents an image of the mid-century seaport in his 1950 woodcut, "South Street." The artist's view presents a solitary tugboat in the foreground, behind which stand a row of four-story slope-roofed buildings facing the East River. Lower Manhattan's skyscrapers and smokestacks fill the background and dominate the skyline. De Pol's burin etches a grey and black sky – we see only slight clearing in the distance –evoking feelings of coldness and dank mist. There are no people in this etching, only the stillness of the buildings and the stillness of the tugboat moored alongside a dock extending like so many of the fingerlike appendages reaching out from the island of Manhattan. A sailboat just barely emerging from beneath the Brooklyn Bridge suggests human activity, yet the lack of any human forms in this image depicts a waterfront that has become desolate and, perhaps, forgotten by the city. By the early 1960s, when several preservation projects meant to commemorate the city's maritime history were in their infant stages, this waterfront scene represented a far cry from the nation's golden age of sail.

THE GOLDEN AGE OF SAIL

By the early eighteenth century, New York City had become the nation's busiest port and was known as the oyster capital of the world. Historically, ours is a maritime nation, and New York City was the capital of this maritime-based prosperity due to its 771 miles of waterfront, clear shipping channels, and a plentiful supply of cheap immigrant labor. In his 1934 survey of the city's seafaring past, *South Street; A Maritime History of New York,* historian Richard McKay declares, "The maritime greatness of New York is its greatest historical asset."[161] His is the master narrative of maritime history that preservation boosters of the 1960s would have known; one would not classify this work as inaccurate, although certainly sanitized and glorified by today's standards in historiography. McKay's narrative provides a history of New York City's shipping trade, shipping magnates and prosperous merchants, from the colonial period to World War I. McKay's history recalls the prosperous days of sail in marked contrast to the author's contemporary landscape dominated, regrettably, by steel and railroad. From his vantage point of the early years of the Great Depression, McKay writes of South Street's heyday, "There was a high tone prevailing at that time, which is now nowhere to be seen."[162]

McKay presents a history of great shipbuilders and shipmasters, from Old John Aspinwall, a sea captain who commanded ships out of New York harbor years before the onset of the Revolutionary War, to the impossibly named Preserved Fish, Junior (son of Preserved Fish, Senior) a senior partner in a packet ship business,[163] to Misters Morgan and Vanderbilt in the mid-1800s, to Mr. William H. Webb, New York City's most famous clipper shipbuilder, who "employed more than a thousand of the most intelligent and skillful mechanics whom the country had ever known, and the East River shipyards often had at the same time twenty or thirty great vessels on the stocks awaiting completion" under his direction.[164] This a history of the great shipbuilding men and merchants who formed the basis of the city's economy in the block surrounding the old seaport, reaching its height of activity and profitability by the middle of the nineteenth century. John Lambert, an Englishman visiting New York in 1807, described the bustling scene along the East River waterfront thus:

When I arrived at New York, in November, the port was filled with shipping and the wharfs were crowded with commodities of every

description. Bales of cotton, wool and merchandise; barrels of pot-
ash, rice, flour, and salt provisions; hogsheads of sugar, chests of
tea, puncheons of rum, and pipes of wine; boxes, cases, packs and
packages of all sizes and denominations, were strewed upon the
wharfs and landing-places, or upon the docks of the shipping. All
was noise and bustle. The carters were driving in every direction;
and the sailors and labourers upon the wharfs, and on board the vessels, were moving their ponderous burthens from place to place. The
merchants and their clerks were busily engaged in their counting-
houses, or upon the piers....Such was the appearance of this part
of the town when I arrived. Everything was in motion; all was life,
bustle and activity.[165]

A year later, our Englishman noted with dismay the effects of President
Jefferson's Embargo Act upon waterfront activity. The Embargo, which took
effect on December 25, 1807, caused a "melancholy dejection" on all activity
and "rendered the city gloomy" until its repeal in March 1809. The War of
1812 likewise resulted in a suppression of port activity, after which shipyards,
wharfs, and merchant activity along the East River and South Street immediately sprung back to life. The returning cacophony of sailors, stevedores,
cartmen, and merchants signaled a flourish of economic activity that would
propel the city forward as the nation's hub of commercial and financial prowess across the century.[166]

Artist William James Bennett's 1834 aquatint of New York's seaport provides a lively depiction of the hustle and bustle of the very district illustrated
in De Pol's 1950 woodcut. "South Street from Maiden Lane," in marked contrast to De Pol's later work, captures the flurry of activity of New York City's
maritime economy, which peaked in activity between 1815 and 1860. Here,
Bennett portrays "a forest of masts" lining the piers of the East River, while
across South Street stand a row of four-story buildings housing grocers, stor-
age facilities, and merchant houses. The street is filled with pedestrians in
fashionable dress, stevedores taking a break from the day's work, men in top
hats and breeches, and horse-drawn carriages ready to load or unload their

passengers. The ships' sails appear awash in sunlight, and the sky is bright with cheer. Bennett's cobblestone streets appear immaculately clean – reality be damned; this is a scene of industry and prosperity and Bennett's intent, or that of his patron, is to depict the East River waterfront as nothing short of glorious.

William J. Bennett, "South Street from Maiden Lane." Aquatint, 1834.
No copyright permissions required, work created prior to 1923 is in the public domain. Per Stanford University Libraries, "Copyright and Fair Use"

For five decades following the end of the War of 1812, America flourished in the shipping trade and dominating shipbuilding and trans-oceanic trade until the start of the Civil War. These balmy years, 1812-1860, marked the true heyday of the city's seafaring economy. State Street, located just opposite the Battery at the tip of Manhattan, offered the stateliest homes for wealthy merchants and their families. These homes enjoyed expansive views of the

New York Harbor and were located mere blocks from the counting houses and mercantile exchanges along South Street. McKay describes these "stirring times," when:

> An old wealthy merchant could get up at daybreak, look out of his window, and see what old cronies were walking upon the Battery. Then he could stroll over before breakfast, and, while enjoying the sea breezes, he would shake hands and talk politics with his constituents, [any one of] the more prominent merchants who then resided on State Street.[167]

McKay's study – a glorified and generally sanitized history to be sure - presents a heroic narrative, complete with strapping men of strength, wit, and wealth. He describes shipbuilders and ship's captains as "men of mark, as well as men of brains and brawn.... Intelligent in trade as in navigation. Life and character and fortune depended on his skill and vigilance." McKay's heroes are the capitalist shipbuilders who built the great merchant vessels, as well as the brave men who officered and sailed those merchant ships across the treacherous seas. Of these men, songs and poems and engravings were commissioned. McKay offers tales of dignity and nobility, men larger than life, the best of the best. Indeed, McKay describes one seaworthy gentleman as "superior to all human beings at that time."[168] Johnny Appleseed and Paul Bunyan most certainly had rivals at the port of New York. These were men who invested wisdom and capital into the very heart of American commerce and industry; the East River waterfront was indeed the very epicenter of mercantile capitalism in a flourishing national economy, captured in one look upon the scene at South Street.

> As one walked up or down South Street, he would be jostled by a continuous stream of men, of wonderful diversity, of every shade of cleanliness, honesty, industry, and intelligence. In fact, every species seemed to be represented.[169]

Map of Lower Manhattan 1835. Drawn by D.H. Burr.
South Street runs alongside the East River, from Coenties Slip on the
lower right tip of Manhattan, to the *Ferry to Brooklyn* and points north.
"The Battery" is the green space at the very tip of the island.

McKay's glowing history of South Street's prosperity only briefly acknowledges trouble on the waterfront amidst these "stirring times." Does a hero
emerge in light of the grittier reality, or despite it? We want to know that our
heroes suffered adversity and overcame despicable hardships. McKay provides
little evidence of this here. Dock thieves and small gangs trolled the docks and
piers in search of an easy mark or cargo left untended. The economic depression of 1857 saw ships standing idle at port for months at a time, during which
time "the working classes were thrown into a state of severe destitution, to
which a long, severe winter added more horrors." At all times, longshoremen

were forced to suffer the shape-up, a demoralizing practice in which a steve-dore hand-selects a few favored men from among a hungry group for load-ing and unloading detail. These longshoremen, "ragged and dirty; they were heavy, lifeless, and even monotonous in various shades of ignorance," hurried to the attention of the approaching stevedore, standing motionless in hopes of receiving the nod of approval and ability to earn a day's pay. The unfortunate majority not selected for work would subsequently disperse into their small groups, relapsing "into their habitual stolidity and inertia."[170] The shape-up would in fact prove to be the bane of the longshoreman's existence well into the twentieth century.

Unbeknownst to McKay's general reader, New York City in fact found it-self in the midst of contention and antagonism during South Street's heyday of industry and prosperity. Of the first four decades of the nineteenth century, historian Joanne Reitano argues, "no other period witnessed so many incidents of violent struggle."[171] The 1830s' surge in immigration caused an outpouring of anti-immigrant, especially anti-Irish Catholic, antagonism. 1834 was the "year of the riots," followed in 1836 by the "year of the strikes."[172] Five Points, New York City's infamous slum and boiling pot of contention in the early nineteenth century, was home to thousands of poor Irish Catholics, blacks, and nativist Protestants. Located behind City Hall and walking distance from the East River waterfront, living conditions in this immigrant ward belied the prosperity marked by the merchant houses along South Street. Five Points would become the national symbol of urban strife and violence, when New York became a pressure-cooker upon an antagonizing sea of change.[173] Due to ethnic and racial conflict, a series of economic recessions, and class strife, the first half of the nineteenth century was plagued by riots, strikes, and violence. In an effort to bring order and sanitation to the dirty and unpaved city streets, officials banned hogs from the streets in 1821, setting off a series of hog riots. From the 1820s to the 1850s, municipal hog catchers snatched untended hogs, inflaming poor New Yorkers who relied on the animals for food and as a source of income, inciting riots. A series of anti-abolitionist riots in July 1834, when anti-aboli-tionists broke up meeting at the Chatham Street Chapel near Five Points, lead to several days of mob violence aimed at black churches, homes, and schools.[174]

1836 was the year of the strikes, in which no fewer than eighteen strikes occurred across the city. Violence erupted in June between two hundred dock-workers and police along the city waterfront; the next day five hundred dock-workers went on strike. Stevedores and laborers, demanding an increase in wages, marched through the streets of lower Manhattan, causing the High Constable of New York to declare, "Gentlemen and Blackguards – Go home or go along with me. 'Tain't no way this to raise wages… make no riots here."[175] On day three, the mayor called in the militia to quell the strike.[176]

New York's waterfront, like much of the cultural landscape at the time, was a racialized space. The Irish dominated waterfront activities around the piers at South Street and on the piers, spreading up both sides of the Manhattan waterfront. By 1850 the New York Waterfront was primarily white and Irish and the International Longshoremen's Association (ILA) was the purview of *white* laborers. Maritime historian Jeffrey Bolster describes that even during the heyday of the nation's maritime trade, "the color line determined what a black man might do aboard American ships." African-American mariners, *Black Jacks*, were generally relegated to work aboard the most dangerous whal-ing ships, which were "dirtier, more dangerous, more estranging, and worse paying than merchant or coastal shipping." Social and occupational mobil-ity remained lateral for most Black Jacks; while a contingency of black sea-men provided fodder for mythmaking and imagery depicting a democratic brotherhood of the sea, the seafaring life rarely propelled the Black Jack out of unmitigated poverty. In light of an entrenched color line aboard seafaring vessels, racism in urban America, and decreasing economic mobility in the antebellum period, black mariners tended to be drifters in and out of the maritime labor market, returning to low-paying and low-status employment on dry land. Coerced labor, threat of flogging, class violence, and racial an-tagonisms created a dangerous environment in which the Black Jack found himself at the utter mercy of tyrannical captains and their officers.[177]

The New York City Draft Riots of July 1863 were fueled by Irish dock-workers' resentment of black "scabs" hired during a labor strike. Tensions be-tween black and white, Catholics and Protestants, aristocrats and laborers, revealed a climate of antagonism in which segments of the city's population squared off against one another. Due to changing demographics, economic instability and a contentious civil war, the cultural landscape of the early to mid-nineteenth century was exceptionally contentious.

FULTON STREET MARKET

Others will see the shipping of Manhattan north and west,
And the height of Brooklyn to the south and east.
Others will see the island large and small;
Fifty years hence, others will see them as they cross,
The sun half an hour high,
A hundred years hence, or ever so many hundred years hence,
Others will see them,
Will enjoy the sunset, the pouring-in of the flood-tide,
The falling-back to the sea of the ebb-tide.

— WALT WHITMAN, *"CROSSING BROOKLYN FERRY"* (1856)

All-night ferry service from South Street across the East River to Brooklyn allowed the Fulton Street Market to operate at all hours of the day and night. In 1816 the city had voted to build a new market along the East River and near the many ferry terminals, replacing several dilapidated structures that had been in operation since the previous century. The Fulton Street Market sold not just seafood, but also beef, mutton, pork, and produce. An account from *Harper's Magazine* in July 1867, exactly one hundred years before the South Street Seaport Museum would emerge, describes the Market as more than a simple fish market, although fish was the raison d'être of the East River marketplace:

Fulton Market is nearly omnigenous. It is a butcher's store, a fruiterer's stall, an oyster-counter, a coffee-shop, a poultry-yard, and a fishmonger's establishment. It is every thing in one – a *magnum* not in *parvo* but a *magnum* in *magno*. It is one vast repository for the sale of every article of diet you could fancy from a lamb-chop up to a 'steak for two,' from a shrimp up to a lobster, from a cup of coffee up to the largest table d'hote fare you could pick out. Fish, however, is its staple article. Fish is as natural in Fulton Market as they are in their own briny element. On fish does Fulton Market especially pride itself with just very reason, and it should be judged by fish alone – its natural belonging, as before observed.[178]

The oyster stall, however, was by all accounts *the* hotbed of activity in the city's seafood trade. In the nineteenth century, one of the highlights of being a New Yorker was the all-night oyster market.[179] As early as 1681, when Britain established a colony in the former Dutch New Jersey, George Carteret reported on the plentiful stock of all varieties of seafood to be found in the New York harbor waterways, including sturgeon, bass, eels, shellfish, and oysters. By 1750, New York was the top city in the colonies for oyster and alcohol consumption. During the Colonial Era, oysters were sold from street carts and from boats moored along the docks at the end of Broad Street. In 1819 the first cannery opened in the city, canning oysters and codfish, to be shipped up the Hudson River and Erie Canal to parts of the country lacking in such sea-riches.

By 1850 New York City was known as having the best oysters in the world, was by this time the greatest port in the world, and was considered the oyster capital of the world. A typical gentleman in 1869 exclaimed, "New York without oysters would cease to be New York."[180] Oyster carts and oyster cellars dotted the city, and could range from high end to questionable. When oyster carts and oyster cellars weren't adequate to sate the appetites of the city's oyster-loving populace, oyster dealers began tying up special oyster barges along the waterfront. Like houseboats, these two-story structures were affixed in a row and accessed by a gangplank from the waterfront. These garish barges were painted pink or yellow or green, complete with ornate decorative roofs and balconies. By 1860, over twelve million oysters per year were sold in the Manhattan markets.[181]

Following the Civil War, shipbuilding and shipping activity fell off dramatically in the United States, serving a keen blow to New York's waterfront activities. Two burdensome federal policies drove this decline. First, the Union Army commandeered all sea vessels during the war for official transport services, effectively eliminating private and corporate ownership of ships and shipbuilding. Second was a shift in federal policy, whereby Southern legislators, intent on crippling Northern powers, engaged in lengthy congressional debates regarding national policy on merchant marines. The resulting legislation cancelled all federal subsidy contracts with the merchant marine industry. These two policies struck a painful blow to the American shipping industry, centered as it was in New York City.[182]

The seaport district surrounding South Street, no longer the epicenter of trade and commerce, began to shrink as shipping magnates left the waterfront in pursuit of continued riches in iron, steel, and the railroads. The waterfront was showing signs of decrepitude, its wooden piers degrading into "rotten structures, the abode of rats and the hiding places of river thieves."[183] With the decrease of industry, South Street, Fulton Street, and State Street became less lively and less fashionable; after the Civil War residents began to move out of the area for more glamorous locations uptown, although the Fulton Market remained active and the all-night ferries to Brooklyn provided a customer base for oysters, coffee, and produce, day and night.

CHANGING NEW YORK

Artist Charles Mielatz captures the late nineteenth century waterfront along South Street in his 1890-91 etching, "Coenties Slip." From the artist's vantage point at the end of the slip, we look upon a row of four- and five-story buildings lining South Street, while dinghies and small sailboats occupy the foreground. The red brick tower of George B. Post's giant Produce Exchange Building reaches into a clear sky marked only by a faint sweep of cloud.[184] The jumbled rooflines of the buildings along South Street create a hodge-podge affair; some of the roofs lay flat, while other slope at impossibly steep angles. Gone are the grand sailing ships of William Bennett's 1834 view. The boats lining this slip are small and squat in comparison; gone too are the stevedores and bustling foot traffic. Untended barrels and crates line the pier, while two lone fishermen sit in the foreground, sharing a single fishing rod, possibly trolling for the day's supper.

Mielatz's etching depicts an East River waterfront past its prime; the bright and prosperous air of Bennett's South Street from a half-century earlier has now become more than a little dingy. Or perhaps Bennett's depiction of South Street merely masked the grime. Bennett's cobbled streets, after all, exist in impossible sparkle and shine; this was the *waterfront,* after all, complete with horse-drawn wagons, fish stalls, sailors who hadn't bathed since who knows when. Mielatz's work offers a more complicated sense of the working landscape which we don't get from the Bennett drawing. There is industry in this visual representation, but little glory. The quietness of the two lone fishermen in the foreground offers a precious form of joy; calm in an otherwise noisy and chaotic city.

Charles Mielatz, "Coenties Slip." Etching, 1890-91.
No copyright permissions required, work created prior to 1923 is in the public domain. Per Stanford University Libraries, "Copyright and Fair Use"

By the close of the nineteenth century, the heyday of the East River seaport had since passed. Writing for the *New York Times* in 1919, the New York art gallery H. Wunderlich & Company comments on the work of Charles Mielatz, noting the artist's focus on forgotten corners of the city and acknowledging this "has less to do with [the locale's] intrinsic merit than with the feeling of place for which Americans are developing as their historic past slips further and further into the background."[185] The public's preoccupation with place and with the past was already lending a nostalgic nod towards an era slowly vanishing. By the turn of the century, remembrance of the city's past as a mechanism by which to shape the urban environment amounted to the first wave of the modern *heritage crusade.* Says historian David Lowenthal, "We long for islands of security in seas of change."[186] The *sea of change* during the Progressive Era applies to an instability associated with political corruption, increasing immigration, entrenched poverty, and public health crises across the turn of the century. Compounding each other, these disturbances added up to a "cultural dislocation" which cried out for historic preservation and the sense of "firmness and stability" it garnered.[187] Progressive Era preservationists fought not only to preserve the city's aging architecture, but to incorporate the historic landscape into a new era of city planning. Historian Randall Mason sees historic preservation during this era as part of the "larger project of transforming the city and its citizens" during an age of social reform. Historic preservation became one component of the civic reform efforts which characterize the early decades of the twentieth century.[188]

Although Wunderlich & Company's astute perception of the public's fascination with place and with history – already evident by the early 1900s - presages our own appreciation for sense of place in the early 2000s, South Street had not quite become a ghostly remnant of its former self. South Street at the turn of the twentieth century still held on to a distinctly maritime ambiance, although admittedly less golden and prosperous than the previous century had witnessed. While the city's infamous oyster market had been shaken – by 1850 New York Harbor's oyster beds had been overharvested and by 1915 the city closed all shellfish beds, including oyster beds, in Jamaica Bay due to sewage contamination – the Fulton Market and South Street were very much alive, if not quite as well. Charles Henry White, writing for *Harper's Magazine* in 1905, offers a flâneur's's rollicking perspective of the busy waterfront:

> Bordering the water-front are the old warehouses and lofts of the sail-maker and boat-builder, with nautical-supply stores and saloons elbowing one another for breathing-space; while stretching out into the river, like long arms, are the massive piers, and moored to these – their quaint figureheads facing the buildings, and their lofty bowsprits half spanning the street – are the deep-sea merchantmen from beyond the seas, with a swarm of stevedores in blue overalls and jumpers bustling about, unloading the cargo and placing it along the waterfront to be loaded on the numerous trucks lined up to receive it...There is an irresistible movement here that is exhilarating.[189]

Throughout the Teens and Twenties, shipping and market activity along the East River waterfront carried on. The Seaman's Church Institute provided a home to sailors moving in and out of the port. Founded in 1834 as a Church of England mission, the Institute at Coenties Slip offered dormitories, reading rooms, postal service, a navigation school, employment and welfare offices to sailors. This boarding house was erected in marked contrast to the many rooming houses dominated by *land sharks*, those seedy characters and thugs who extorted wages from sailors and kept these seamen locked in an insufferable cycle of poverty and misery. Richard McKay described those illicit rooming houses as purveyors of:

> The vilest dens, the deadliest rum, the basest companions, gamblers and women, lodgings in cellars where no human being ought to have been kept, bad literature, bad songs and corrupting music, held as in chains of steel the New York sailor.[190]

Sailors could rent a room on the cheap at the Institute, without the fear of extortion or robbery that typified less reputable rooming houses. While the dormitory might assault the olfactory lobes with its pervading odor of men who have been long out to sea, and would likely appear rather brusque to the gentle visitor, these were mere inconveniences. The transient schedules of the sailors and their constant inter-mingling with an "army of bums and panhandlers" who also found sanctuary in the building ensured the clientele was, while perhaps not of the gentle class, able to get a good night's sleep, send and receive mail, and seek employment services.[191]

FRAUNCES TAVERN

A short walk west from the Seaman's Church Institute leads one to the corner of Pearl and Broad Streets at the tip of lower Manhattan. Located at this intersection is Fraunces Tavern, perhaps best known as the site of General George Washington's farewell address to his staff upon his giving up command of the Continental Army on the night of December 4, 1783. The Tavern was built as a family home in 1719 for Etienne De Lancey, a French Huguenot merchant. No known images survive of the original three-story brick structure, but written descriptions of the home recall its design, quite vaguely, "in the British taste." As the neighborhood became increasing commercial, the De Lancey family moved out of the home to a more fashionable location uptown, after which the building was used as an office and warehouse for the mercantile firm of Delancey, Robinson & Company.

In 1762, West Indian Samuel "Black Sam" Fraunces purchased the building and opened the Queen's Head Tavern, named after King George III's wife, Queen Charlotte. Samuel Fraunces had a personal and professional relationship with General George Washington. During the Revolutionary War, Fraunces' daughter Pheobe served as General Washington's housekeeper at his Mortier house on Richmond Hill. November 23, 1783's Evacuation Day elicited cheers from the New York citizenry, when General Washington led his officers into Manhattan, ceremoniously driving out the British troops who had occupied the city during the Revolutionary War. Although military engagements had ceased two years prior, the Definitive Treaty between Great Britain and the United States was not signed until September 3, 1783 in Paris.

The treaty officially ended the Revolutionary War and called for the evacuation of all British troops from their hold on the Empire City.

On the evening of December 4, 1783, New York State's first Governor, George Clinton, entertained Washington and his troops at Fraunces Tavern, where Washington gave his infamous and emotional farewell address to his officers in the Long Room. Samuel Fraunces renamed the tavern after himself following this auspicious occasion; Queen's Head Tavern no longer seemed appropriate. In 1789, Washington returned to New York City as President of the United States, and asked Fraunces to serve as steward in his presidential household. When the federal government moved its offices from New York to Philadelphia the following year, President Washington asked Fraunces to join him yet again. Samuel Fraunces died in 1795 and the Fraunces Tavern was sold in 1801.

The building saw a number of real estate transactions exchange its ownership across the next century, and by 1900 the building was threatened with demolition to make way for a modern skyscraper. The Sons of the Revolution, a patriotic order founded in 1883 in the Long Room one hundred years after Washington's speech there, tried to purchase the property and were rebuffed. The group joined forces with the Daughters of the Revolution and with Andrew H. Green, president of the Society for the Preservation of Scenic and Historic Places and petitioned the city for an injunction.

In 1903, the City Board of Estimate and Appropriation passed an ordinance to buy the building and save it from condemnation; the Sons negotiated a contract and purchased the Tavern in 1904. By this time, interest in preserving the building was considerable, with both the Sons and Daughters of the Revolution joining efforts to preserve the building associated with George Washington and his heroism and leadership during the fledgling days of the new republic. This was the Progressive Era, when historic preservation became part of the larger urban reform movement intent on building a modern city and creating better citizens through a determined reorganization of the built environment. Progressive Era reformers sought to solidify social and cultural identity through the physical and aesthetic landscape of the city. Shoring up the cultural authority of the nation's founding fathers was motivated by the social, economic, and political challenges of the rapidly industrializing city.

Immediately, the Sons hired architect W.H. Mercereau to begin restoration efforts on the Tavern. The Sons' goal was to restore the building "to what it may well have looked like" when Samuel Fraunces ran the Tavern from 1762 to 1785, and this thus became the New York City's first historic restoration project.[192] A series of fires in 1832, 1837, and 1852 significantly altered the appearance and structure of the building and in 1890 the first floor of the building was actually removed in order to lower the first floor to the ground level. By the turn of the twentieth century, the building represented a veritable storehouse of memory, although its eighteenth century structural "authenticity" was questionable.

The series of fires across the mid-nineteenth century had severely altered the building from its original construction, including its height and roofline. In addition to the lack of any certain imagery of the building's original appearance, these fires further complicated any understanding of what the original structure purchased by Fraunces may have actually looked like. Mercereau began the restoration by removing the fourth and fifth floors, which had been added to the building over the course of the nineteenth century, and reconstructed the roof line based on imprints the original roof line had left on a neighboring building. In 1907, the newly renovated Fraunces Tavern opened to the general public. Over the next several decades, the Sons acquired several other properties on the block, thereby resisting the commercial redevelopment, if only quite locally, that would transform the landscape of lower Manhattan across the twentieth century.

LANZA'S FISH MARKET

The Fulton Fish Market still engaged in big business, raking in an annual income of $18-20 million in 1931 and second only to Billingsgate of London in the global fish trade. When a 125-foot section of the Market collapsed into the East River in 1936, newspaper reports assured concerned New Yorkers that fish shortages would not occur: fish deliveries would be re-routed to safe piers until the structure was rebuilt. New Yorkers continued to love their sea-food and the Fulton Market, by now receiving the majority of seafood by truck instead of by boat, was still a flurry of activity, a mélange of sights and smells and the site of "bewildering traffic." Eels wriggled across slippery floors, lobsters escaped from open traps, nosey turtles wandered from the turtle bin, across the market floor, and into somebody else's business. Owing to the frantic pace of seafood deliveries, New Yorkers were kept in fresh supply of mackerel, eel, shad, bluefish, catfish and scallops. The oyster's numbers had dwindled significantly.

By the 1930s frequent fires, union strikes, and charges of racketeer-ing dominated any discussion of South Street and the Fulton Fish Market. Reports on waterfront blazes generally acknowledged these fires originated with "causes unknown." According to Commissioner of Markets William F. Morgan, Jr., the 1933 repeal of Prohibition led to a major spike in rack-eteering in other New York City markets once the repeal put bootleggers out of business. In the interwar years, an ethnic shift had taken place in which Italian-American dockworkers outnumbered the long-entrenched Irish on the New York waterfront everywhere except Manhattan's West Side. Mob con-trol at the Fulton Fish Market dates back to the 1920s, when Joseph "Socks" Lanza, a capo of the Luciano (originally Morello, later Genovese) crime fam-ily, established himself as boss of the United Seafood Worker's, Smoked Fish and Cannery Union Local 359. "Not a scallop moved through the place that Lanza did not profit from."[193] Lanza controlled all aspects of the fishing trade, including loading and unloading all fish at the Fulton Market; fisherman crews were not allowed to unload their own catches, instead required to pay a fee for "public loaders" to the union's benevolent fund. Lanza's control of the Fulton Fish Market served as the Genovese crime family's revenue and power base and was an "intractable fact of life" during his reign.[194]

In 1931, a federal investigation into charges of racketeering at the Fulton Fish Market fell under the direction of Special Assistant to the Attorney General, Albert J. Law. In June 1933, two union heads at the Fulton Market were indicted under the Sherman Antitrust Act. Charles Skillen, president of United Sea Food Workers Union, and Lanza, business agent of the union, were indicted by a grand jury on counts of extortion and coercion after individuals from Connecticut trucking companies had testified the men had demanded payment of $50 and $100, under threat of bodily injury, before they could transport their cargo to the Market. Later reports uncovered a history of payoffs for "protection" at the Market, with the Fulton Market Fish Mongers Association acknowledging for the past six years it paid $5,000 in "protection" fees annually to an organization referred to only as "they." In addition, every boat was required to pay a $10 unloading fee at the South Street piers.[195]

While serving a two-year sentence on the Sherman Antitrust conviction, Lanza, self-proclaimed Czar of the Fulton Fish Market, pleaded guilty to a similar charge in the saltwater fish market, for which he received an additional one-year prison term. After serving his time at Leavenworth federal penitentiary, Lanza returned to New York and was reelected to his post as business agent of Local 16,975 of the United Sea Food Workers Union. In a story not uncommon to many an underworld crime drama, Lanza immediately faced new charges of extortion upon his return home, when union officers claimed he had continued to extort $120 per week from Teamsters members while he was incarcerated at Leavenworth. In January 1941, "Socks" was arrested on these new charges at his racketeering headquarters in the old Meyers Hotel at Peck Slip and South Street, after which he was committed to the Tombs and later sentenced to 7 ½ to 15 years. Parole officer Abe Simon later acknowledged, "The market should be called Lanza's Fish Market. Fulton Fish Market is a misnomer."[196]

Mobster control notwithstanding, the Fulton Fish Market occupied "one of the liveliest places in New York" and fulfilled the city's and the country's insatiable demand for seafood. Following the 1936 collapse of a dilapidated portion of the market into the East River, a new facility re-opened in June of 1939, although the modern amenities and "new orderliness" were not necessarily welcomed by every old-school fish monger. In keeping with the modernist push for order and rational use of space, the new building would better serve the ongoing shift from sea to surface traffic; by this time 85% of all fish to the market arrived by truck or by rail, and traffic congestion around the market was insufferable. In fact, Mayor Fiorello LaGuardia ordered a stop to the open-air sale of fish at Fulton Street, much to the dismay of the fish-monger community, claiming the curbside selling of seafood had created an intolerable traffic hazard.

By 1945, five million pounds of seafood entered and left the Fulton Fish Market every week. New York continued its long tradition as seafood purvey-or and connoisseur; the nineteenth century oyster cart and oyster barge sellers would have been pleased. When a fire, of undetermined origin, broke out on the roof of the Market and affected an entire block at South, Fulton, Beekman and Front Streets, fish sellers and their customers on the street level continued to conduct business as usual while firefighters battled the blaze on the roof.

DOWN AT THE OLD FISH MARKET

Joseph Mitchell, writer for *The New Yorker,* spent many mornings wandering the streets, fish sheds, and waterfront along the Fulton Fish Market in the 1930s, '40s and '50s. With the majority of commercial maritime traffic now engaged along Manhattan's West Side and New Jersey's Hoboken piers across the Hudson River, activity at South Street and the Fulton Fish Market would only become increasingly anachronistic. A throwback. A backwater. The bottom of the harbor. The Fulton Fish Market, buried beneath the Brooklyn Bridge and the regular foot traffic that characterized lower Manhattan's typical weekday rush, became Mitchells' destination of choice. The writer's colorful depictions of this salty locale added to the mythology, collective meaning, and placemaking of the old cobbled seaport. Mitchell writes of the downtown backwater, "The smoky riverbank dawn, the racket the fishmongers make, the seaweedy smell, and the sight of this plentifulness always give me a feeling of well-being."[197] Mitchell captures the vanishing – not yet deceased - life of the fisherman, the sea captain, and the fishmonger, and illustrates what the seafaring life around the harbor had dwindled to by the mid-century.

By the 1920s and '30s, oyster harvesting around New York Harbor suffered under a number of factors which compromised the city's long-standing designation as oyster capital of the world. Large-scale oyster industry, with its machinery and dredging equipment, squeezed out the old oysterman and his manually-operated oyster rake; contaminated waterways presented a public health hazard – "bad" oysters were implicated in outbreaks of typhoid fever - and required the shut-down of oyster beds across several decades; the dredging of channels for larger ships destroyed oyster beds around New York waterways; and natural seedbeds gave out due to overharvesting. The once-bountiful New York oyster, traditional foodstuff of street carts and oyster cellars, had become an expensive delicacy.

One of Mitchell's real-life literary characters included fisherman Archie M. Clock, commander of the *Jennie Tucker,* "a battered, stripped-down, thirty-eight-foot sloop powered with a motor the Captain took out of an old Chrysler."[198] Captain Clock descended from a long line of fishermen and oyster farmers: his forefathers trolling the waters of Long Island Sound for two centuries. Clams – Clock no longer trolled for oysters - harvested from the waters of Long Island Sound and South Bay were taken to the Fulton Fish Market and to restaurants in Manhattan and Brooklyn, or trucked to the Campbell's Soup factory in Camden, New Jersey. The process of getting fresh clams to market had not changed much over the past century. After the clams were harvested, they were poured into wire baskets and dipped into an antiseptic-infused solution for cleaning. Loaded into three-bushel barrels and three-peck tubs, the catch was then delivered to the Fulton Fish Market and local restaurants for eagerly awaiting customers.[199]

Saltwater farmers like Captain Clock were part of the thriving fish business around New York harbor in the 1930s and '40s, but one increasingly dominated by large-scale industry. In 1938, General Foods Corporation harvested, canned, and shipped approximately 100,000 gallons of shucked oysters from the waters surrounding New York Harbor. Servicing the best oyster farms in the world, Mitchell describes 25,000 fishermen at work - hauling, shoveling, culling and shucking oysters.[200] Transporting this seafood to the City was itself no small feat, whether mobsters grabbed you in a shakedown or drunks blocked your way during the pre-dawn trek into Fulton Street. Captain Clock recounted to Mitchell a typical journey with his partner, trucking in from Long Island to the Fulton Market, where upon "entering South Street, he had to climb out of the cab and drag a sleeping drunk out of the road. Truck drivers have to slow-poke through here just because of drunks. I drag one out of my way at least once a week."[201]

Sloppy Louie's was Joe Mitchell's restaurant of choice, a "busy-bee" establishment, mere steps from the old Fulton Market along Schermerhorn Row. With a clientele consisting primarily of fishmongers and fish buyers, but including a growing number of folks from the nearby financial district, the joint was packed on any given day. The line of lunchtime latecomers waiting for a table usually got on proprietor Louie's nerves. Mitchell describes a typical Sloppy Louie's customer through a composite sketch he calls Old Mr. Flood, a man who rises to greet the market every morning before the crack of dawn, drinks his coffee black, has a morning smoke, and enjoys his daily stroll through the fish stalls and oyster sheds. The fictional Mr. Flood, perhaps Mitchell's own alter ego, recalls those flâneurs of the last century, who wandered the bustling seaport in all manner of exuberance and satisfaction.

Through his meanderings around the seaport and along the East River and Hudson River waterfronts, Joe Mitchell portrays the lived reality of a dwindling community of fishermen and the fish trade as they existed in the 1930s, '40s and '50s. These essays describe a very particular sense of place in the decades approaching the mid-century. It is important to note that Mitchell's essays do not engage with the criminal element thoroughly ensconced at the waterfront, including "Socks" Lanza's racket at the Fulton Fish Market, or the occasional dismembered body discovered by junk collectors in the predawn hours, or the shakedowns along the Hudson River piers. Mitchell writes with a pen meant to enchant. What he offers his reader is a literary depiction of a dwindling community of local fishermen, with the implication that *this* was the seafaring heritage of old New York. While the seaport at South Street, the eateries along Schermerhorn Row, and the fishermen and oyster shuckers who brought in the catch continued to exist in various manner of hustle and bustle, Mitchell's nostalgia for the past to which these cling is palpable. Mitchell depicts a fish market still "quivering with life," presents a cast of characters whose vibrancy and intrigue added to public perceptions and helped to create meanings associated with a South Street past its heyday but still tethered to another era.

ON THE WATERFRONT OR THE OLD MAN AND THE SEA

By the mid-1950s, while Joe Mitchell was wandering through the old seaport, Fulton Fish Market remained a profitable industry contained within the larger commercial activity at the Port of New York. The Market processed over 250,000,000 pounds of seafood per year, operating in much the same manner as fishermen of the 1840s would have known. With only five percent of seafood now arriving by boat, the majority of the Market's wares arrived by truck, including such diversities as Cuban swordfish, Florida red snapper, Alaskan king crab, German brook trout, Canadian sturgeon, South African lobster tail, and Indian shrimp. Employing approximately two thousand fishmen swinging baling hooks and hatchets, and sales clerks yelling out transactions in code, the Market tallied a $125 million per year business and in the predawn hours was "quivering with life against the backdrop of a still sleeping city."[202]

However, the Port of New York, including the Hudson River waterfront and the East River waterfront in both Manhattan and Brooklyn, had become by this time an "outlaw frontier... where criminal gangs operate[d] with apparent immunity from the law."[203] Malcolm Johnson's Pulitzer Prize-winning investigative series "Crime on the Waterfront" ran in the *New York Sun* in late 1948 and exposed the gritty realities of what the waterfront had become. New Yorkers, their legislators, and Hollywood were captivated by the series.

Criminal activity on the waterfront was not new to 1948. Crime had been a festering sore within New York City's markets since the repeal of Prohibition. Little or nothing, Johnson reported, had been done about it. After the end of World War II, crime on the waterfront escalated such that mobsters now controlled all aspects of the port's commerce and activity. Kickbacks, the loading racket, pilfering, entire truckloads of cargo gone missing, and all other forms of corruption drove the cost of business at the New York port to unsustainable heights. As a result, many shipping companies had begun to divert their business to other ports along the eastern seaboard, where loading and "protection" fees did not exist.

Mobsters controlled all aspects of longshoreman activity through the union, with known criminals appointed as hiring bosses and union officials. The Czar of the Fulton Fish Market, "Socks" Lanza, still in prison, nonetheless continued to control the piers of lower Manhattan and the Fulton Fish Market through his lieutenants on the outside. Johnson declared, "The law on the waterfront is essentially the law of the jungle. It's every man for himself." [204]

The "shape-up," that demoralizing practice carried over from the previous century and outlawed in London and other U.S. ports, was still in use in New York. Longshoremen were required to gather on the piers at 7:00 am and again at 1:00 pm, forming themselves into a horse-shoe, waiting obsequiously in the hopes of receiving one of the few coveted brass tickets doled out by the hiring boss which would allow the man to work a half-day shift. This practice, rife with graft and favoritism, was the root of evil on the waterfront, keeping the men in a state of perpetual job-insecurity, provoking antagonism and a man-against-man mentality, and requiring men who did not get a day's work to borrow from the ever-present loan-sharks, members of the same mob controlling the International Longshoremen's Association, who in turn garnished the laborer's next day's pay.[205]

In addition to the shape-up, longshoreman suffered the kickback, in which each man was required to pay the hiring boss a 10% fee for the privilege of being chosen during the shape-up. Finally, the loading racket, which was institutionalized at the Port of New York after World War I, required that all incoming cargo must be loaded onto trucks via "public loaders" - members of the ILA – with "loading fees" paid directly to the racket bosses. Truckmen were not allowed to load or unload their trucks using their own loaders, finding it safer to suffer the extortion than to sit with a load of cargo that did not move. Intimidation tactics ensured that everyone followed procedure or suffered the consequences. This was business.[206]

By the mid-century, a crew of mob bosses – Irish, Italian, and Sicilian - controlled the waterfront on both sides of the Hudson and East Rivers. Mickey Bowers ran the Hudson River piers along Manhattan's West Side; Tim O'Mara ran the piers from 42nd to 14th Streets; John M. Dunn, in Sing Sing awaiting his sentence to the electric chair, controlled the piers below 14th Street; "Socks" Lanza controlled the piers of lower Manhattan and the Fulton Fish Market; Albert Anastasia controlled the East River and South Brooklyn piers. Their boys controlled each and all activity on the piers, including the loading and un-loading of trucks, shylocking, bookmaking and kickbacks. New York District Attorney Frank Hogan claimed the New York waterfront produced more murders per square foot than anyplace else on earth. While a certain exaggeration, the rampant violence and death on the waterfront had become so familiar; it was impossible to determine which victims were the results of mob violence or the usual gang warfare.

Elia Kazan's film *On the Waterfront* was released in 1954, based on Budd Schulberg's screenplay which itself was based on Malcolm Johnson's 1948 "Crime on the Waterfront" expose. The film, starring Marlon Brando, Karl Malden, and Eva Marie Saint, received twelve Academy Award nominations and won eight, including Best Motion Picture, Best Actor, Best Supporting Actress, Best Director, Best Story, and Best Screenplay, and launched Marlon Brando into the Hollywood stratosphere. *On the Waterfront* riveted audiences one year following a very different maritime-based work of literature, Ernest Hemingway's book, *The Old Man and The Sea,* for which Hemingway won both the Pulitzer and Nobel Prizes, and the subsequent film starring Spencer Tracy. These two works, each critically and popularly acclaimed in the early 1950s, illustrate at once the romance and brutal agony tied to a life of the sea, and present a stark juxtaposition between man's romance with the sea and the reality of a crime-infested and racket-ridden waterfront.

Written in the great tradition of maritime-inspired prose, in which the romantic lure of the sea is equaled to the devastating trials of bravery a life upon the sea demands, Hemingway's tale follows the works of writers such as Herman Melville and Joseph Conrad, who write of heroism and human fate at sea. *Moby-Dick* stands out as the epic tome of man's trials upon the sea, however when Melville's tale was originally published in 1851, it was met with little popular interest. Literary critic Carl Van Doren's 1917 essay, published in the *Cambridge History of American Literature,* renewed interest in Melville's tale for a twentieth century audience. Van Doren, hailed as "one of the most brilliant critics of his day,"[207] proclaims *Moby-Dick* one of "the greatest sea romances in the whole literature of the world," and describes Melville as a transcendentalist and a romantic, a writer who filled his classis work with "moral or poetic significance."[208] As *Moby-Dick* began to receive both critical and popular acclaim following Van Doren's essay, we must ask: what questions were early-twentieth century modernists posing, and what answers were they seeking, in Melville's *Moby-Dick*? On the fundamental meaning of *Moby-Dick*, Van Doren describes an eternal conflict between man and nature:

> The chase after Moby-Dick comes to have the semblance of a conflict between the eternal, unscathable forces of nature and the ineluctable enmity of man; and the eventual catastrophe, which leaves ship and sailors strangling in the water while the great beast shoulders his white way off on other business, seems the crash of a tumbling order.[209]

More recent literary criticism on Melville's work concurs. Richard Brodhead praises Melville's literary strength in creating "the power and presence of the full-fledged heroic self."[210] Brodhead describes the tale as "outrageously masculine," a tale that illustrates for its readers a fantasy of what it means to be a man. Captain Ahab joins the rank of other literary giants like Hamlet, Lear, and Oepedis, heroes who "sum up some fact of human potential and bare the contours of some exemplary human fate."[211]

Melville's other well-praised tale of the sea, *Billy Budd*, tells the story of a fated sailor, consigned to the sea and later to death, caught up in the naval wars between France and England. Set in 1842, *Billy Budd* is a tale of good versus evil, innocence versus "malice, envy, and spite." Melville wrote *Billy Budd* in the late 1880's, a period of cultural turmoil and unrest. Historian Alan Trachtenberg agrees that Melville's work offers a social commentary on the author's own time, finding the similarities between the novel and Melville's own historical moment of widespread unrest, challenges to government and authority where issues of morality and legality were settled only by authorized force, are too great to ignore. Billy Budd, the "Handsome Sailor" and the embodiment of mortal goodness, is the tale's hero, a hero who stands up "against the receding utopia of the rights of man." Melville's symbolism and allegory help to fuel the reader's understandings of Melville's own social landscape, and provide insights into the larger societal questions with which Melville grappled.[212]

Some recent literary criticism seeks to complicate the traditional wisdom on *Moby-Dick* and *Billy Budd,* uncovering the novels' "infrapolitics" and nuanced narratives. Sterling Stuckey's *African Culture and Melville's Art: The Creative Process in Benito Cereno and Moby-Dick* uncovers the influence of African culture on Melville's life and work. Literary historian Wai Chi Dimock's *Empire for Liberty: Melville and the Poetics of Individualism* views Melville as social critic and seeks to uncover the "dialogic relation" between Melville's work and the social landscape of the nineteenth century.[213] While adding to the reader's understanding of Melville's personal influences and his work as a social critic, neither of these arguments negate the traditional interpretation of *Moby-Dick* and *Billy Budd* as tales of heroism. Each of these literary critics – from Van Doren to Trachtenberg to Stuckey - remind us that the writer's cultural landscape, as well as the larger questions posed by his reader, provides insight into the meanings imbedded in and ascribed to literature, and helps to clarify *why* these meanings resonate with different audiences at different times.

Hemingway's *The Old Man and The Sea* continues in this tradition of heroic and maritime-inspired literature. Unlike *Moby-Dick, Old Man* was an instant success from the moment it was released. When *LIFE* magazine first serialized the story in its September 1, 1952 issue, 5.3 million copies sold within the first forty-eight hours. Scribner published the book the following week, where it remained on the best-seller list for six months. While some critics have faulted the tale for its unabashed sentimentality, such criticisms exist in the minority. The tale is most frequently described as brilliant. Upon the book's publication, literary critic Leo Gurko praised Hemingway's "incurable reliance on the individual," and tied *The Old Man and The Sea* to the works of Melville and Conrad. Gurko dubs old man Santiago as "the clearest representation of the hero... heroic even in his bad luck." True heroism, according to Gurko, is tested mano-a-mano; when the fight comes, one must face it alone. For the hero does not *share* his agony. As one man battling one great fish, old man Santiago exudes the deepest sense of heroism in a world where there are two kids of men: the greater man, and the lesser. The alpha and the beta.[214]

More recent literary criticism on *The Old Man and The Sea* confirms prevailing wisdom that Hemingway's tale embodies the quintessential modern classic about courage and strength. Whether he wins the struggle or loses it, Santiago's battle against his adversary "raises him to a higher plane of *dignity and pride.*" His heroism comes from his unwillingness to concede and his willingness to endure until the battle has ended. One way or another. Santiago's struggle is a universal one; his fight against the great marlin and the sharks that thwart his efforts represents an epic struggle for survival. And so while Santiago's adventure occurs in the tropical waters off the coast of Cuba, his trials represent a "permanent and universal challenge, that of life itself."[215]

Literary critic William Cain finds prevailing themes of "majesty and the pointlessness of human effort" in Santiago's tale. In light of this pointlessness of effort and the assurance of death, the question Hemingway poses, is: *how should we live?* What is a dignified life? What does heroism and strength look like? *The Old Man and The Sea* is at once a simple tale of heroism and perseverance upon the open sea, yet at the same time illustrates the "theater of cruelty" that is life. Hemingway's tale explores the fundamental question, *what is life, in the midst of adversity and death?*[216] As Santiago endures his battle with the great fish, "the reader revisits ideas about what makes a man."[217]

Hemingway's old man Santiago represents an archetype, an iconic and idealized symbol of the pre-industrial seaman – a character not unlike the hard and tough seamen we meet through Joe Mitchell - who would later be commemorated at South Street. Santiago's dignity and heroism conjure the historic landscape from which such heroism emerged, in the days before steel and iron and mobsters and rackets invaded the nation's maritime trade. By the American mid-century, seafaring men like Santiago had long since become a myth, an ideal. And yet, Santiago embodies a lasting vision, which, at the mid-century, recalled an era belonging to a different breed of men.

In *The Old Man and The Sea,* Hemingway presents one man and one fish, locked in a battle of wills and strength. The book's hero, Santiago, lives a traditional fisherman's life on the coast of Cuba, in a simple shack not far from the water's edge. Santiago fishes for his supper every day and owns few worldly possessions: his boat, the mast, and his fishing gear. The old man tends to the stations of his cross like every other fisherman in the village, and like their fathers and grandfathers before them.

Hemingway speaks to the romantic associations that tie man to the sea. He writes that Santiago:

> Always thought of the sea as *la mar,* which is what people call her in Spanish when they love her... The old man always thought of her as feminine and as something that gave or withheld great favors, and if she did wild or wicked things it was because she could not help them. The moon affects her as it does a woman, he thought.[218]

Santiago's quest, to land the massive marlin on his hook, leads him further and further from shore, well into the night and the following day, a relentless pursuit in a battle of wills. The fish is noble and dignified; this is an honorable endeavor and a trial of strength. Santiago honors his adversary, assuring the fish he had never seen a more beautiful or graceful creature

When sharks begin to seek out Santiago's catch, this huge marlin larger than the boat to which it is strapped, the old man knows he is in for a battle. The shark is fearless and will take what he wants without hesitation. The sharks threaten the old man's work, profit, and glory. They will steal from him. Once the first shark approaches and tears away a chunk of the marlin, Santiago knows that more sharks will soon follow the scent of the fish's blood, and he "knew that a very bad time was coming...They were hateful sharks, bad smelling, scavengers as well as killers."[219] The old man knows the sharks will get the better of him and his fish; he cannot fight them all. Even an old man such as Santiago has the strength and fortitude to engage in battle one-on-one; yet against a school of sharks, he knows he will be beaten. While the sharks succeed in robbing the old man of his prized marlin and of his glory, Santiago drags his exhausted body back to shore to rest and to live to fish another day.

A hero who stretches his powers of strength and will to the limit, Santiago exercises freedom of action. This heroic tradition in writing disappeared from

Western literature after World War I, when it was replaced by Kafkaesque protagonists who lack this freedom of action.[220] Santiago's agency upon the open sea epitomizes the myth of the heroic seaman. It is of no consequence whether Santiago exists off the coast of Cuba, or New York, or Nantucket; Hemingway captures the romance of the sea and evokes a *traditional* fisherman's life. Santiago is an archetype and an allegory. He is master of his own ship and of his own fate; he harkens back to a different breed of men. Bernard Berenson, art connoisseur and cultural aficionado whose discriminating eye dominated the art world across the first half of the twentieth century, described *The Old Man and The Sea* as "an idyll of the sea as sea." And while Hemingway vehemently denied *Old Man* was about anything more than one particular man battling one particular fish, Berenson complicates the what-you-see-is-what-you-get assertion with astute literary criticism: "No real artist symbolizes or allegorizes… but every real work of art *exhales symbols and allegories.*"[221]

LIFE magazine serialized *Old Man* in 1952; Scribner's published it later that same year. Hemingway's Santiago personified freedom of action for his readers and would provide a stark contrast to the downtrodden longshoremen depicted in Kazan's 1954 film *On the Waterfront*. Where Hemingway tells the romantic story of one man battling one fish, a man living a fish-to-market existence much the same as generations of fisherman would have experienced before him, Kazan depicts the criminality of contemporary waterfront life, where longshoremen do not work for themselves but are at the mercy of mobsters and institutionalized corruption seeking to destroy man's dignity. A close examination of these concurrent works reveals a representation of the 1950s' waterfront in marked contrast to the romantic mythology of the traditional seaman's life and the glory of the sea. Understanding the juxtaposition of these artistic productions highlights the notion of a usable past at the South Street Seaport. Commemoration at South Street would reject everything the contemporary crime-ridden waterfront had become – everything Johnson and Kazan depict *On the Waterfront* - while bringing to life the strength, honor, and humanity of the preindustrial seaman's life as romanticized in Hemingway's tale.

On the Waterfront begins with longshoreman Brando's Terry Malloy, leaving Longshoremen's Local 374 with a cadre of thugs in tow. We see Terry approach an apartment building where he shouts from the sidewalk, "Hey, Joey!" As Joey appears from an upstairs window, Terry releases a homing pigeon to its rooftop coop. Heading to the roof to retrieve his bird, Joey suddenly falls six stories to his death. Terry looks completely bewildered, naïve in his mumbling, "I thought they was going to talk to him...I figured the worst they were gonna do is lean on him a little bit..." During the ensuing investigation with local police, the victim's mother cries that her son was the only longshoremen gutsy enough to talk with federal investigators about the crime on the waterfront, and everybody knew it. An older longshoreman coming to check out the crime scene tells his buddy, "I've been on the docks all my life, boy, and there's one thing I learned. You don't ask no questions, you don't answer no questions, unless you wanna wind up like that." A pigeon's death.

As the story unfolds, we learn that mob boss Johnny Friendly controls all waterfront activity through the union local and is currently under investigation by the federal Crime Commission. Friendly explains to Terry that his crew takes its cut from everything that moves in and out of "the fattest piers and the fattest harbor in the world." Sensing Terry's dismay over the murder of his friend, an indignant Friendly shouts, "you don't suppose I can afford to be boxed out of a deal like this, do you? The deal I sweat and bled for, and I got one lousy little cheese-eater, that Doyle bum who thinks he can go squealing to the Crime Commission, do ya?"

In a scene right out of Malcolm Johnson's expose, longshoremen fight one another like dogs at the morning shape-up. Father Corrigan, local pastor and moral authority, is filled with righteous indignation at the site of this dehumanizing treatment. Father asks the men who have been shut-out from a day's work, "well what about your union? No other union in the country would stand for a thing like that!" To which a disaffected longshoreman replies, "The waterfront's tougher, Father, like it ain't part of America."

You've got to be D&D on the waterfront – deaf and dumb – if you want to survive. Everyone knows it: the mobsters know it, the longshoremen know it, readers of Malcolm Johnson's expose know it, and now Hollywood and the

American audience know it. When word gets out that another longshoreman, Timothy Doogan, has spoken with federal investigators, Johnny Friendly instructs his henchmen, "We got the best muscle on the waterfront and the time to use it is now, pronto, if not sooner." Later, a load of crates is dumped on Doogan while he works in the cargo hold of a ship and the "pigeon" is killed. This latest act of intimidation and murder compels Father Corrigan to deliver his real-life alter ego's infamous "Jesus is in the shape-up speech." Father councils the men, "only you, with the power of God's help, have the power to knock 'em out for good." This is a moral crusade, one that demands collective action and public outrage to silence – for good! – the cowardly and un-Christian mobster vice that has corrupted the good people of the waterfront for generations.

After Terry testifies against Johnny Friendly in court, Edie finds Terry on the rooftop and cautions him: it's no longer safe for you here. In the film's dramatic conclusion, Terry seeks out Johnny Friendly on the dock, where the two men fight, mano-a-mano, until Terry gets the better of the mobster and Friendly's thugs are called in. Terry is beaten to a pulp while the union can only look on. Father Corrigan appears, helps Terry up, and challenges our hero to "finish what you started," go in there and take back the union from the thugs. Terry staggers up the pier, bloody and unstable. He stumbles up to the shipyard entrance, right up to the shipping owner who stands in front of his enterprise and, impressed with Terry's fortitude and moral strength, shouts "Let's get to work!" The longshoremen pour in for a day's work, Friendly has lost control of the local. Terry and his moral high ground are victorious. The waterfront has been reclaimed, at least for these men. It is possible to fight corruption and reclaim an honest space.

On the Waterfront is a tale of corruption and exploitation, and ultimately of heroism and personal vindication against larger forces. Kazan's longshoremen experience indignity as they grovel for work and for their livelihood. Based on Johnson's *New York Sun* expose, this film offers a tale of the longshoreman at the mid-century. Revisiting De Pol's 1950 woodcut of South Street, we can easily place Terry and his fellow longshoremen within that dank and somber landscape, although not so easily in Bennett's earlier and quite cheery vision of waterfront prosperity. *On the Waterfront* presents a dramatic illustration of New York City's gritty and crime-ridden seaport at the mid-century.

Heroism, dignity and agency characterize Hemingway's Santiago and recall nineteenth-century sailors and seamen, full of bravado and strength. Where was heroism, dignity and agency along the mid-century's racket-ridden waterfront? What had once represented the capital of capitalism among the nation's ports during the profitable Age of Sail had deteriorated, by the mid-century, into the racket-ridden domain of organized crime where seamen and fishmongers eked out a living only by the grace of men more powerful than they. McKay bemoaned the loss of our nation's maritime prowess in the wake of the Civil War; the twentieth century had been no kinder to New York's waterfront. When McKay elicited his call to action, "Americans, east, west, north and south, must be ship-minded, incurably maritime!" he may not have known the call would be taken up by the historic preservation movement thirty years later. Following the shipping industry's shift to containerization in the 1960s and with the issue less about shipping as industry and fundamentally about identity and collective memory of New York's maritime greatness, the battle of the port would be one of representation and perception. The heroism of a Terry Malloy or Old Man Santiago might still be found along the city's aging waterfront, and New York's greatest historical asset might yet be located in its maritime history.

Chapter 4

BATTLE OF THE PORT;
PRESERVATION AND COMMEMORATION
AT THE SOUTH STREET SEAPORT

*Any landscape is composed not only of what lies before
our eyes, but what lies within our heads.*[222]

— *D.W. Meinig, "The Beholding Eye" (1979)*

It comes as no surprise that by the late 1960s, diverse communities of Americans were looking for a moral authority they could believe in. The decade's increasingly volatile early and middle years necessitated a response to the question, *what sort of people are we, we Americans?* The police riots and attacks on civilian demonstrators during the 1968 Democratic National Convention were, perhaps, the culminating manifestation of a systemic fracturing of any perceived sense of national ideology, identity, or consensus, and indicated a gap that spanned much more than the generations. From Muhammad Ali to Neil Armstrong to Marlon Brando, a nation searched for heroes. Simon and Garfunkel, hipster folk-rockers of the Sixties and Seventies, sing of the nation's lonely eyes searching for heroes. Even baseball great Joltin' Joe DiMaggio had left the scene. Our heroes had gone away.[223]

The broad cultural landscape from which any generation seeks its heroes is home to people, places, and events both present and past. In light of the social reality of the present, memories stored in the cultural landscape of the past take on a heightened, even mythologized meaning. And while Malcolm Johnson's 1948 expose had shone a very bright light on the widespread criminal activity monopolizing New York City's waterfront, ten years following a citywide investigation along the waterfront, a city crime commission reported, "The hoodlums never went away." Through the 1960s, the Mafia continued its steady presence on the waterfront, and was now affiliated with Jimmy Hoffa and his Teamsters Union. Rampant pilferage, cargo gone missing and the ever-present loading racket continued to plague the waterfront.[224] If, as historian Richard McKay declared, New York's greatest historical asset was its maritime greatness, what did the current infestation of crime on the waterfront say about the city's identity?[225]

The story of historic preservation in 1960s' New York City is not simply about bricks and mortar. It is about memories and pride.[226] When supporters of preservation and commemoration in lower Manhattan – from Peter Stanford to Whitney Seymour to David Rockefeller to the Sons of the Revolution - looked across the physical landscape, they each saw not only what lay before their eyes, but what lay inside their heads. Questions seeking solutions. The resurgence of this preservation impulse was part of a larger gestalt of the era, in which the tenuous notion of a collective identity fractured under the weight of domestic unrest and a questionable foreign policy. Led by South Street Seaport Museum founder Peter Stanford, preservationists at South Street sought to "revive mythical values" amidst a cultural landscape in which crises abound.[227] Historian James Lindgren, who has conducted a complex organizational history of the South Street Seaport Museum, characterizes the city's cultural landscape during the Museum's founding years as one that was widely fractured.[228] Lindgren describes the motivating sensibilities behind the Friends of South Street, in which nostalgic notions of a more heroic past mingle with Progressive Era reformists' vision for an improved civic landscape. In seeking to build a sort of homage to the past at South Street, these men and women saw nineteenth century windships as symbolic of a *better time*, and believed that through the careful refurbishment and presentation of these vessels, they could teach Americans some very fundamental and essential lessons about how to move forward. Lindgren astutely discerns that "Myths, nostalgia, and wishful thinking partly shaped Seaporters' perspectives, but they were as much concerned about bettering their own world as lamenting the lost past."[229]

While critics of the city's crooked streets and muddled arrangement found fault with the nineteenth century's lingering effects on the cityscape, preservationists at South Street meant to preserve a small remnant of the previous century's character and, perhaps, charm. The physical transformations wrecking havoc on the city's nineteenth century landscape threatened to eradicate this "more natural" human scale; this has become the conventional wisdom explaining the preservation impulse during the age of urban renewal. However, upon closer examination of internal memos, personal conversations, and museum proposals surrounding the plans to commemorate the Age of Sail in lower Manhattan, we find a much deeper tie, amongst "the people of our generation," to notions of resuscitating a more noble – indeed mythical - identity in the midst of an unwelcome meaninglessness of the age.[230]

Beyond the urge to buffer – not halt - the physical reconfiguration of lower Manhattan, a wide-ranging group of preservationists envisioned commemorative projects dedicated to remembering the strength and heroism of the city's preindustrial maritime roots and the people who built that cultural landscape. The actions of historic preservation supporters of the late 1960s demonstrate for us today the values by which they lived and the ideals they privileged. In the midst of a physically and morally deteriorated waterfront, and in the context of the 1960s' cultural revolution in all of its manifestations and implications, New York City's existing waterfront represented the wrong sense of place for a growing body of historic preservationists, the financial community, and nautical aficionados. However, good intentions alone do not guarantee a successful outcome in the process of historic preservation. Bricks and mortar, real estate and renovation, come at a price both political and financial. Supporters of South Street, fueled by memories and pride, would have to battle for their right to the port.

What groups identify and sanctify as their pasts
becomes historical evidence about themselves.[231]

— *DAVID LOWENTHAL (1979)*

"THIS GODDAM CRAZY BILL"

As the oldest district of one of the nation's oldest cities, lower Manhattan and the area surrounding New York Harbor had become, by the mid-1960s, a neighborhood rich with commemorative sites. A look at the National Register of Historic Places lists Castle Clinton National Monument, originally called Fort Clinton and the site of the nation's first immigration center, as a national historic site in October 1966. That same month Federal Hall National Monument, site of President Washington's inauguration, was listed to the Register, as was the Statue of Liberty National Monument, Ellis Island, and Liberty Island. Earlier in 1966, the nearby U.S. Customs House announced its impending move from Bowling Green to the future World Trade Center, and the 1907 Cass Gilbert structure was named to the National Register. Following the 1965 formation of the City's Preservation and Landmarks Commission under Mayor Wagner, lower Manhattan – site of the city's earliest settlement - was slowly becoming an epicenter of public commemoration, bursting with the power of place.

In 1966, New York Senator Whitney Seymour Jr. introduced a bill to the State Senate that would create a State Maritime Museum in lower Manhattan. During his tenure as President of the Municipal Art Society, Seymour had noted with alarm the encroachment of the urban renewal bulldozer across the island of Manhattan and the trail of destruction left in its wake. In an article written for the *New York Times* in late 1963, Seymour pleaded with the city to curb the bulldozer and spare at least some remnants of the Georgian and Greek Revival structures that had survived since the nineteenth century. Presaging historian Max Page's work on the creative destruction of Manhattan, Seymour cited capitalism's demands for an ever-increasing productive use of land as the reason behind the endless razing and rebuilding of the city's landscape. Seymour voiced a public plea in the form of an open letter to the *New York Times*, in which he heralded the buildings along South Street as some of the few extant vestiges of New York's greatest asset: its harbor and port. In his "Plea to Curb the Bulldozer," Seymour called for a halt to the planned destruction of the federalist era structures along South Street, suggesting the buildings might be saved to house a maritime museum.[232] Three years later, the newly elected junior senator introduced his bill for the creation of just such a museum.

Seymour's bill quickly passed both the Senate and Assembly, and was put before Governor Nelson Rockefeller for approval. Governor Rockefeller's brother, Chase Manhattan Bank Vice Chairman David Rockefeller, was strongly opposed to the maritime bill. David Rockefeller had founded the Downtown-Lower Manhattan Association in 1958, whose mission was to support the physical expansion of the financial district. When the D-LMA got word that "this goddam crazy bill" – Seymour's term - had passed both houses, a flurry of protest was directed at the Governor's office.[233] According to a *New York Times* article, David Rockefeller's personal appeal to the Governor contained such heated objection to the maritime museum that many who read the letter were alarmed by the "violence of the attack."[234] President of the D-LMA Edmund Wagner's own appeal to the Governor reveals the reasoning behind his organization's opposition to the development of the Seaport area for museum purposes, and highlights the tensions between those who admired the last century's nobility and those who admired the next century's tax base.

STRONGLY OPPOSE SENATE [bill] 3524 AWAITING YOUR SIGNATURE. SENATOR SEYMOUR, WHO INTRODUCED THE BILL, WELL-INTENTIONED BUT ENTIRE CITY BLOCK IN LOWER MANHATTAN, TOGETHER WITH FULTON FISH MARKET AND ADJACENT PIERS, LAND AND WATERFRONT PROPOSED FOR SOUTH STREET MARITIME MUSEUM, COULD BE USED BETTER FOR NATURAL EXPANSION OF FINANCIAL AND INSURANCE COMMUNITIES. CITY WOULD BENEFIT GREATLY FROM

ADDITIONAL REAL ESTATE AND BUSINESS TAXES THAT
COMMERICAL STRUCTURE COULD PRODUCE. BILL IN
APPARENT CONTRADICTION WITH CITY PLANNING
COMMISSION PLAN FOR LANDFILL DEVELOPMENT AND
DEPRESSED HIGHWAY ALONG EAST RIVER. MUSEUM
PROPOSAL MIGHT CONFLICT WITH PLANS FOR
RESTORATION OF FRAUNCES TAVERN BLOCK.[235]

Likeminded letters of protest from stakeholders in Manhattan real estate,
the chairman of that competing historic preservation project at Fraunces
Tavern, and a variety of corporate lawyers soon joined opposition from David
Rockefeller and the Downtown-Lower Manhattan Association.

At the root of this opposition were three words synonymous with real
estate investment: location, location, location. A historic museum located
in the financial district was fundamentally viewed as an affront to the "orderly and dynamic growth of lower Manhattan," and specifically as infringing
upon the physical expansion of the financial industry in the years to come.[236]
John Goodman, Executive Vice President of the D-LMA, argued on behalf
of the downtown financial community, insisting the city would lose big in
unrealized tax revenues if the nonprofit maritime museum were approved.
As a nonprofit organization and therefore exempt from city real estate taxes,
Goodman estimated a loss of $30,000 per year to the city. On the other hand,
Goodman argued, if the proposed maritime museum block was "developed
to its best potential," it could produce up to $300,000 per year in property
tax revenue for the city. Goodman further acknowledged the maritime museum project would be in direct competition with a museum block project already under development just steps from South Street, known as the Fraunces
Tavern Block.[237]

Stakeholders at the D-LMA met with Senator Seymour in the hopes of
reaching an amicable solution for the completion of two historic preservation
projects on the table for development in lower Manhattan. Goodman regret-
ted that a common ground proved elusive. Supporters of both the maritime
museum and the Fraunces Tavern museum block were equally determined to

see their project's fruition. At South Street, supporters at this juncture were few, but included Senator Seymour, a grassroots cadre of seaport fans known as the Friends of South Street, shipping magnate Jakob Isbranstsen, the editors at *Popular Boating* magazine, and the *New York Times'* architectural critic Ada Louise Huxtable. Support for the Fraunces Tavern museum block was more widely garnered across both civic and financial communities, and included the Sons of the Revolution, David Rockefeller and the Downtown-Lower Manhattan Association, real estate developers Atlas and McGrath, the City Parks Commission, the City Planning Commission, the City Landmarks Commission, the City Board of Estimate, and the Museum of the City of New York. Furthering the protest against Seymour's maritime museum legislation, a letter from one local real estate firm to Governor Nelson Rockefeller suggested if Senator Seymour insisted upon his "romantic museum," proving a complete disregard for the interests of "every knowledgeable, interested and responsible person who lives and works downtown," the museum might alternately be established north of Fulton Street, on less valuable real estate.[238]

Not content to allow his maritime museum to suffer at the hands of fraternal alliance, Seymour composed his own letter to Governor Rockefeller, in which he reiterated the importance of preserving New York City's maritime heritage and reaffirmed the economic benefits that could be reaped from the museum endeavor. "I know your brother is opposed to this legislation," wrote a seemingly defiant Seymour to the Governor, "and he probably recommended to you that you veto it. But I urge you to disregard him, and do the right thing and sign the bill."[239]

The D-LMA was the sponsor behind the 1966 groundbreaking of the World Trade Center and beyond that massive project, had proposed a series of redevelopment plans for the area. In addition to commercial redevelopment strategies intended to revive the flagging financial center, the D-LMA was a primary supporter of the already in-progress Fraunces Tavern museum block restoration project, located a short walk from the proposed South Street site. David Rockefeller and the D-LMA, while vociferous in arguing for the commercial expansion of lower Manhattan's valuable real estate market as the ultimate goal of the area's redevelopment, nevertheless had plans of their own for heritage commemoration at Fraunces Tavern and the integration of a "usable past" in redevelopment of the financial district.[240]

FRAUNCES TAVERN

Plans to create a museum block surrounding Fraunces Tavern became public record in late 1963 when James Grote Van Derpool, Executive Director of the City's Landmarks Preservation Committee, released a "Preliminary Proposal for the Development of the Fraunces Tavern Block as a Historic District" on November 26. The plans called for a total of eight buildings to be restored on their original locations, four buildings to be moved from Whitehall and Front Streets and restored on the museum block site, and a reconstruction of the seventeenth century Dutch Stadt Huys. The restored block would house a maritime museum, a financial museum, a merchant's house museum, as well as the renowned Fraunces Tavern.

Rationales for the museum block project included the desire "to assure a worthy memorial to the early trading, shipping, banking, professional and family interests of the city," to "memorialize worthy chapters in the early life of our city," and to "add a warm humanizing element to the region which would commendably enhance the public image of downtown New York and the great business interests it represents."[241] Clearly, this project was a business venture meant to commemorate the city's commercial history, steeped as it was in the shipping and mercantile trades. The project commemorating the history of capitalism and free trade had the backing of David Rockefeller personally – coming from a family well-versed in the philanthropic arts and Colonial Era heritage commemoration - as well as the combined support of the D-LMA.[242] David Rockefeller, feeling the dis-ease associated with the urban crisis and mounting "societal ills," felt a personal and institutional responsibility to address the social and financial crises that plagued the nation.[243] Public commemoration at Fraunces Tavern of the memory and heroism of the nation's founding fathers corresponded nicely with Rockefeller's mandate to engage Chase Manhattan Bank and the downtown financial community in philanthropic and other cultural endeavors. In 1965, the year before Senator Seymour introduced his maritime museum legislation, the City's newly formed Landmarks Preservation Commission granted landmark designation status to Fraunces Tavern, although this designation did not affect the entire museum block project's chance for success. The LPC's authority was still relatively new and meager and could not safeguard any surrounding properties, however the Sons of the Revolution's ownership of the Tavern provided a sense of assurance that its survival, if not that of the entire block, was secure.

While the D-LMA's opposition to Senator Seymour's legislation argued the "real purpose" of Seymour's bill was "to preserve a small group of run-down old buildings on the south side of Fulton Street now used for miscellaneous commercial purposes,"[244] plans for the Fraunces Tavern museum block were presented as a *scholarly project* spearheaded by the Museum of the City of New York's newly formed Downtown Museum, "in order to enrich the public appreciation of the history of the City of New York, of its early government, of its growth as a world center of commerce and finance, and of the character of its streets and buildings."[245] With estimated project costs at $5,000,000, almost $37,000,000 by 2015 standards, the project would include the relocation of four historically significant buildings currently residing at Front and Whitehall Streets. So while the D-LMA presented the Fraunces Tavern museum block project as a scholarly endeavor dedicated to enhancing the public good, it derided Seymour's Maritime Museum legislation as detracting from valuable real estate development better suited to the expanding financial community.

A series of early nineteenth century three- and four-story brick structures built in the Federal and Georgian styles had once been the elegant homes of some of the city's prominent merchant families. Located on the site of a proposed new Stock Exchange, these architectural remnants of the city's balmy Age of Sail - now in "crumbling, peeling shambles" - were threatened by the proposed widening of Water Street as part of the Stock Exchange Urban Renewal Plan. Commercial developers Atlas–McGrath owned the buildings in question and had agreed to donate the deteriorated structures and relocate them to the Fraunces Tavern block, once other – less desirable and architecturally significant – buildings currently occupying valuable space on the Fraunces block could be razed. McGrath did not shy away from displaying blatant skepticism over the intended move, telling the *New York Times* the plan was simply "a joke." McGrath's professional opinion was that the aging and very dilapidated structures would likely crumble with the first attempts at relocation.[246] A rebuilt version of the original Dutch Stadt Huys and the four merchant homes would join Fraunces Tavern and five additional properties owned by the Sons of the Revolution in the creation of a seventeenth-to-nineteenth century museum block conglomeration. This potentially dubious reconstruction, undertaken "from available documents," would create an "entire block, including its surrounding sidewalks and street lights [and] provide a full scale, authentic and dramatic illustration of two-hundred years of New York history."[247]

Not everyone felt the historic authenticity of Fraunces Tavern or its proposed museum block was a worthy project. To Ada Louise Huxtable, legendary architecture critic for the *New York Times,* the reconstruction of Fraunces Tavern amounted to "preservation gone wrong." With her usual candor, Huxtable deplored what she saw as an act of historic fabrication, an increasingly prevalent situation in which reconstruction only served to diminish the value of the original. In one particularly scathing article, Huxtable characterized the ever-increasing propensity to destroy original buildings in favor of rebuilt imposters as "galloping restorationitis…Across the country the genuine heritage of the nineteenth century is still being razed to be replaced by elaborately rebuilt synthetic eighteenth-century stage sets more pleasing to the twentieth-century taste." The originator of this horrendous disease, this galloping restorationitis, was none other than the Rockefellers' very own Colonial Williamsburg, which Huxtable classified as a sham of historical merry-making, amounting to nothing more than "historical play-acting," where real treasures and modern fakes stood side-by-side so that no one knew what *authentic* even meant.[248]

Citing the Fraunces Tavern museum block project as part of this insufferable malady, Huxtable claimed the museum block would require such a thorough reconstitution of the buildings that the recreations would be indistinguishable from Fraunces Tavern, itself already a make-over project from 1907. Next to nothing of the original eighteenth century tavern, claimed Huxtable, survived. Hammering the final nails into the coffin, Huxtable challenged, Fraunces Tavern "is not old, it is not authentic, and under no circumstances is this kind of thing preservation."[249] A follow-up response in the form of a letter to the editor challenged Huxtable's dismissal of Fraunces Tavern, claiming many of the Tavern's original structures were in fact salvaged, and those parts that were rebuilt were "as authentic as research can make them." Further, the letter argued *the significance of Fraunces Tavern was less in its architecture per se and more directly located in its association with George Washington.* Claiming the last word, Huxtable agreed that the present iteration of Fraunces Tavern might in fact contain some *associative* historical value, although the distinction between a true architectural remnant of history, and a restoration-reconstruction-fabrication, deserved serious consideration.

The Fraunces Tavern Controversy of 1965 exposes a valid argument: while objects, including architectural structures, can serve as symbols of conscious or unconscious value systems and may constitute symbols of power or prestige, and while architectural styles have the ability to suggest societal ideals through their aesthetic design, at what point is an object or building rendered no longer *authentic enough* so as to compromise these very mechanisms at play? Does Fraunces Tavern's authenticity retain its value if 80% of the interior and exterior construction has been rebuilt? What happens at 90%? Does the retention of the building's original frame and support beams satisfy our totemic desires, or do we require that the original floorboards of the Long Room, upon which General George Washington bade his officers farewell, remain intact in order to absorb that intangible goodness and integrity from the earlier era? If, as philosopher-writer de Botton argues, the power of architecture lies in its ability to *suggest* a moral message or cultural ideal, how might the careful restoration or re-creation of the original structure alter that message?

The Downtown Museum of the City of New York, organized to orchestrate and direct the project, requested the City fund one-fifth of the total project cost *if* $2,000,000 could be successfully raised from private sources.

David Rockefeller had personally contributed $50,000, about $350,000 in 2015 dollars and a rather small drop in the bucket in terms of Rockefeller family wealth, in start-up costs. In addition, the DMCNY estimated an annual operating budget for the museum block at $227,000 and requested the City provide $127,00 of those annual funds, "based on the formula established for other museums."[250] At a planning meeting in the Office of the Borough President of Manhattan on July 26, 1966 – one week before Governor Rockefeller would either approve or reject Senator Seymour's bill for a state maritime museum to be located at South Street - the Fraunces Tavern museum block project received optimistic support from the Borough President of Manhattan, the City Planning Commission, the Landmarks Preservation Commission, Community Planning Board Number One, the Downtown Museum of the City of New York, the Park Department, the Downtown-Lower Manhattan Association, and the Sons of the Revolution.

Under the terms of its proposal, the Fraunces Tavern museum block would be designated a city park and operated as a museum by the Downtown Museum of the City of New York under the jurisdiction of the Department of Parks for administration and maintenance. The City's Capital Budget for 1967-68, under Mayor John V. Lindsay, included funds for the project and included $1,350,000 in capital investment tethered to private funding secured from outside sources.[251] Supporters of the Fraunces Tavern project feared Senator Seymour's Maritime Museum plan would deplete fundraising opportunities and be in direct competition with the maritime and other house museums planned at the Fraunces site. MCNY's Chairman, Louis Auchincloss, composed his own letter of opposition to the South Street proposal.

While Seymour's vision for South Street conjured images of the lost days of nineteenth century sail, the Fraunces Tavern project presented an equally ennobling narrative of the patriotic Revolutionary War era. And while the South Street Seaport Museum would focus attention on interpreting the lives of tradesmen, stevedores, laborers, women, and Black Jacks, with Fraunces Tavern's exhibitions interpreting a more traditional historical narrative of the great men who led the young nation to independence, both visions ascribed to lower Manhattan a narrative steeped in personal and collective heroism.

This narrative particularly alluring during a time when the nation's identity was challenged from abroad during a political and cultural race to win the Cold War, and challenged domestically amidst the growing dissent of the Civil Rights movement, anti-war protest, and counterculture challenges to the Establishment and status quo. What the Friends of South Street saw in their vision along the East River seaport, Fraunces Tavern supporters conveyed through their own preservation project: each project located heroic memories in the physical landscape of the city as a means to foster civic identity and pride in a national heritage.

The D-LMA's primary objection to the Seymour legislation concerned the loss of commercial real estate and future tax revenues to the City with a nonprofit organization occupying valuable downtown property. The organization was also concerned that the creation of a historic museum at South Street would prove redundant to its own plans to move forward on the Fraunces Tavern block and create competition among private funding sources. Despite this opposition, Governor Nelson Rockefeller, steeped in a tradition of Rockefeller family philanthropy, approved the New York State Maritime Museum legislation on August 2, 1966 *after* Senator Seymour, rattled that the growing opposition to his legislation might result in its gubernatorial rejection, removed all wording for the appropriation of any public funds towards the maritime project.

Victory for Seymour's Maritime Museum legislation prompted the Friends of South Street to organize and focus on fundraising for ship restoration and real estate acquisition at South Street. Friends of South Street constituted an energetic grassroots movement, an entirely separate entity from the newly appointed Maritime Museum, although conceived with a shared purpose of maritime commemoration along the East River waterfront. Three months later on November 29, 1966, the Manhattan Community Planning Board Number One voted in favor of the Fraunces Tavern museum block project. With the City's pledge to allocate funds– funding the South Street project was *not* entitled to - and inspiration drawn from the "authentic and scholarly" restoration of Colonial Williamsburg as its guide, plans for the restoration of the Fraunces Tavern museum block forged ahead alongside development plans

at the South Street Seaport. From the start, these competing plans for commemoration of the Age of Sail atop the pricey values of lower Manhattan real
estate begged the question: how much heroic national identity and character
can one city privilege over the riches of real estate development?

Competing visions of heroism. The first image is located in 1783, the second in
1861; both long removed from 1967 and commemorative projects at Fraunces
Tavern and South Street, and both emanating from cultural landscapes themselves
marked by strife and war. At the same time, both images represented, to
supporters of the Fraunces Tavern museum block and the South Street Seaport
Museum, a time steeped in ideals of personal and collective heroism.

"George Washington bids farewell to his trusted and dedicated officers at
Fraunces Tavern," Fraunces Tavern Museum (Left); J. Morgan, "The Storm At
Sea," originally published in *Illustrated London News*, Nov. 23, 1861 (Right)
No copyright permissions required; works created prior to 1923 are in the
public domain. Per Stanford University Libraries, "Copyright and Fair Use."

GETTING BACK TO FUNDAMENTALS

In 1966, nautical aficionado Peter Stanford was writing ads for Beefeater Gin
at the Madison Avenue agency of Hicks & Greist. His father was a trustee of

the Mystic Seaport in Connecticut and had been commodore of the Cruising Club of America; *TIME* magazine had described the young Stanford as "a seadog" practically from the time he could walk.[252] Stomping around many of the same haunts frequented by Joe Mitchell at the old Fulton Fish Market, Stanford and his wife Norma had a personal affection for the seafaring life and its vanishing imprint on the urban landscape. Stanford, who characterized himself as "a conservative, rational, and outraged American," nevertheless held fast to romantic ideals for a better future, a hearty appreciation for the democratic values of ancient Greek civilization, believed in the social reform legacy of the Progressive Era, and questioned much of Progress' incessant and ever-determined push forward.[253] Conservative and idealist at once; much like the historic preservation movement itself.

In 1961, urban journalist and Greenwich Village resident Jane Jacobs published *The Death and Life of Great American Cities*, a work widely regarded as spearheading the post-modernist transformation in urban planning. In a voice echoing Jacobs, Stanford recalls the cobbled streets and sloped-roof buildings around the aging seaport embodied a much needed and "more humane" scale than was evident in the rapidly multiplying barren plazas and stark skyscrapers of lower Manhattan. When a fellow nautical-buff alerted Stanford to Senator Seymour's maritime museum legislation very recently passed into law by Governor Rockefeller, Peter and Norma arranged a meeting with the Senator at his downtown office. Seymour explained to the Stanfords the extent of the new legislation, which included the creation of the New York State Maritime Museum, allowed the state to acquire the buildings along Schermerhorn Row but did not provide any funding for their acquisition or rehabilitation, and authorized a governing board which would seek funding to purchase the site and undertake all necessary renovations.

Following this meeting, the Stanfords immediately organized the Friends of South Street, a separate grassroots organization created to support the development of Seymour's Maritime Museum and to expand the vision at South Street. It is important to note, this grassroots up-start was not directly tied to Seymour's Maritime Museum; the organizations would have separate missions and operating structures and the New York State Maritime Museum only ever really existed on paper. Within a handful of years, what remained of the State Maritime Museum's rather impotent board would be absorbed by the South Street Seaport, when a final bond measure to ensure its continued support failed to pass.[254] The primary purpose of the Friends of South Street was to tell the vernacular history of South Street in its heyday, restore the vanished image of wind ships to the lower East River waterfront, and preserve the Federalist style buildings that lined the streets.[255] According to Stanford's vision for the Seaport, this historic district would encompass a working community of tradesmen, shops, and ship restoration activities, each contributing to the ambience of the seaport's cultural landscape and revitalizing the city's maritime heritage.

The Friends' response to the proliferation of cement and steel superstructures transforming the landscape of Manhattan took a hearty cue from urbanist Jane Jacobs' sidewalk ballet and urban critic Lewis Mumford's writings on the city as a social construct. In this regard, and like Progressive Era preservationists before them, Seaport boosters harbored a belief that preservation of the physical and cultural landscape would foster a climate of civic engagement during an era of cultural dislocation, and also envisioned ways in which preservation might be integrated into the larger project of urban planning. Stanford equated the South Street Seaport with a modern Greek agora, a civic meeting space in which urban dwellers would gather in democratic discourse and make real, human connections.[256] Stanford and the Friends of the Seaport believed a community of maritime-related shops, museums, cafes, and working tradesmen would provide an economic benefit to the city. They envisioned a new urban future in which South Street would become an economic as well as aesthetic asset to the city, predicting a blend of small shops and entertainment activities would promote real commerce in an authentic maritime atmosphere.[257]

In addition to the physical preservation of Schermerhorn Row, Stanford was concerned with creating a viable economic asset similar to the economic successes realized by San Francisco's Ghirardelli Square revitalization project.[258] Following the suggestion of City Commissioner of Marine and Aviation Herb Halberg, who advised Stanford to secure personal support from the Rockefellers, Stanford composed a letter to Warren Lindquist at

Chase Manhattan Bank, in which he requested the D-LMA's (*read:* David Rockefeller's) support of the Seaport plan. In this, Stanford argued for South Street's role in the larger project of the financial district's redevelopment, remarking "[The Seaport plan] does not subtract one inch of commercially valuable land for lower Manhattan. It simply enriches open space set aside in the Lower Manhattan Plan."[259]

New York City however was not Mystic, Connecticut, or San Francisco's Ghirardelli Square, two maritime preservation projects Stanford knew well. The demands and challenges of one of the world's largest cities presented financial realities unequalled in the seaport restoration communities Stanford loved. The vision for this seaport district would have to confront the unique demands created by the economic and political climate of mid-1960s Gotham, where lower Manhattan real estate was valued among the world's priciest and the financial district was regarded as the Capital of Capitalism.[260]

"ONE YEARNS TO REARRANGE THE HODGE-PODGE AND PUT THINGS WHERE THEY BELONG"

The Friends of South Street needed the support of lower Manhattan's financial community in order to gain favor with the City Planning Commission and the Board of Estimate and secure stewardship rights to the highly valuable real estate just east of the city's financial district. This meant obtaining the support of David Rockefeller, the financier personally concerned with addressing the larger societal ills associated with the urban crisis and presently backing the Fraunces Tavern museum block project. Social consciousness aside, economic vitality in lower Manhattan was a priority for Rockefeller and the D-LMA, which had been actively working on a series of redevelopment plans for the expansion and support of the financial district for well over a decade. The expansion of lower Manhattan's financial district was a serious obstacle confronting commemorative plans at South Street. In order to manifest the myriad aspirations for this commemorative landscape, in order for the revitalization of values and heroes and memories to see the light of day, the incessant needs of Manhattan real estate development demanded attention.

To understand the ideologies fueling mid-century urban renewal and the D-LMA's vision for commercial revitalization in the 1960s, we have to look back to the early decades of the twentieth century, when emerging visions in urban planning characterized lower Manhattan, as well as downtown districts across the country, as a chaotic hodge-podge in need of systematic reorganization and "morally uplifting" architecture.[261] Historian Eric Darton explores the trajectory of modern urban planning, which has been heavily influenced by the prevailing vision of early twentieth century urban theorists who demanded the chaotic hodge-podge of the nineteenth century city be scrapped in order that a rational, centralized plan be implemented.[262] In the wake of the Progressive Era's City Beautiful movement, which called for large, centralized architecture and the orderly configuration of urban space, The Regional Plan Association, through its *Plan for New York and its Environs*, recommended strategies for the recentralization of financial and commercial industries as well as the optimization of zoning and land use through more efficient and rational use of space.

In 1922, the Regional Plan Association was formed in New York City with the objective to create a comprehensive survey of the region. From 1927-1931, the RPA proposed several public works projects and land use strategies, including new highway patterns, bridges and tunnels, and skyscrapers with expansive street-level plazas in order to open up congested city streets. The RPA's position was that misuse of land was the root of all the city's problems, including the belief that the wrong sorts of buildings for the wrong sorts of purposes were occupying prime real estate in the city. The presence of industrial factories and tenement housing in the middle of prime real estate offended the sensibilities of the RPA, which argued, "Such a situation outrages one's sense of order. Everything seems misplaced. One yearns to re-arrange the hodge-podge and put things where they belong."[263]

The modernization and rationalization of New York City's physical landscape during the 1930s and 40s followed RPA guidelines for commercial development and infrastructure improvements such as highways, bridges and tunnels. A major turning point in land use development came in 1949, with Title 1 of the American Housing Act. This "federal bulldozer" legislation authorized federally subsidized clearance of undesirable, underutilized, and undervalued land.[264] City Construction Coordinator Robert Moses, the most infamous of twentieth century urban renewal icons, was especially adept at using the combined powers of eminent domain, Title 1 slum clearance, and rational city planning to eradicate the jumbled architectural landscape of the nineteenth century and replace it with LeCorbusian "towers in the park."[265] Underscoring the political as well as economic motivations behind mid-century urban renewal, historian Samuel Zipp reveals the political ideology behind the city's makeover during the Cold War years. Moses and his supporters were interested not only in developing commercially profitable properties, but equally concerned with creating a gleaming, modern cityscape to symbolize the supremacy of American capitalism during an ongoing and heated ideological battle with the Soviet Union.[266] Nineteenth century quaintness, however nostalgic or sentimental, had no functional or ideological place in the modern economy of the city.

Lower Manhattan's mid-century financial troubles date back to the Great Depression. The area experienced its first wave of skyscraper construction in the early twentieth century, but the collapse of the nation's economy in 1929 left the financial district stagnant for the next two decades. By the end of World War II, over 80% of the buildings in lower Manhattan had been constructed prior to 1920, most neither fireproof nor modernized.[267] As the district was littered with industrial manufacturing lots, produce and food markets, and fringe tenement housing, many banking and other financial institutions fled for more modern accommodations in Midtown, where construction and redevelopment had already gained momentum. As banks, law firms, and financial institutions moved uptown, an aggressive plan for lower Manhattan's redevelopment was seen as a critical factor in saving the district from further blight. When David Rockefeller announced plans in 1955 to build Chase Manhattan Bank's new headquarters near the Battery, a strategy for the future of lower Manhattan materialized. In addition to its own super-block construction, Chase funded several other new downtown projects in accordance with the D-LMA's recommendations set forth in its 1958 report, the Lower Manhattan Recommended Land Use plan.

The 1958 plan, which would be known as the First Report in a series of four over the next fifteen years, presented an analysis of land use, traffic patterns and suggested physical improvements to the area. The D-LMA's series of reports did not suggest what form new development would take, rather the plans recommended optimum use of land and resources. The physical design of downtown's makeover was left for future consideration. Critical to the report's recommendations was its assessment that areas surrounding the financial core of lower Manhattan were in a state of decay and deterioration, occupying valuable land that would be better served by direct support of the financial industry. The area just south of the Brooklyn Bridge, where the future South Street Seaport might emerge, was slated for middle-income residential development, intended to house financial sector employees as a "walk to work" locale. Mayor Wagner and the City Board of Estimate quickly endorsed the plan, hailing it as much needed and long overdue. The D-LMA's Second Report, presented in 1963, reaffirmed its earlier recommendations for land use, adding that blight along the East River waterfront, from the Brooklyn Bridge to Battery Park, should be converted to a pedestrian esplanade. This recommendation for recreational waterfront usage was not entirely dissimilar to Stanford's vision for a walk onto the piers amidst the open sky and waterfront.

The D-LMA's recommendations for land use and commercial development were given physical shape and form with the Lower Manhattan Plan of 1966. While four decades of regional planning and commercial construction had altered the landscape of lower Manhattan, many of the D-LMA's recommendations to expand the financial district and increase residential housing had yet to be realized. Proposed as a comprehensive redevelopment scheme that would support the growth of the financial district with multiple residential complexes, pedestrian-only thoroughfares, altered traffic patterns and a recreational waterfront, this dynamic new vision, The Lower Manhattan Plan, was presented to the New York City Planning Commission. While Seymour's Maritime Museum and Stanford's Seaport district were in their fledgling stages, the financial community of lower Manhattan was eagerly awaiting the City's approval of the most expansive redevelopment plan to date.

Echoing the earlier 1958 plan presented by the D-LMA, The Lower Manhattan Plan remarked on downtown's inability to compete with midtown's "rich diversity of facilities." Although the decade had seen a marked increase in office space downtown, employment in the area actually declined from approximately 400,000 in 1960 to 375,000 in 1965. This trend was startling, in light of the increase in office space that resulted from the creation of Chase Plaza and other modern skyscrapers that had been erected since 1960. By 1966, plans for the construction of the World Trade Center were well underway, in which an additional 7.6 million square feet of office space would soon become available. Dilapidated piers, elevated expressways cutting the city off from its rivers, inadequate parking, and poor use of space were unsightly detractors from the area's financial core. The plan proposed expansion of this business core in order to create a "strong physical impact on the area" and attract new businesses to occupy the World Trade Center as well as the current surplus of office space downtown. Critical to the Plan was the proposed creation of a desirable upscale housing market. Six waterfront residential clusters - to house 80,000 to 100,000 people - were designed, situated along waterfront plazas and connected by an esplanade.

Fulton Street was earmarked as the northernmost residential cluster along the East River, just south of the Brooklyn Bridge - the site of the proposed South Street Seaport Museum. All but two buildings in the proposed South Street Seaport district, which would receive its charter within months of the Lower Manhattan Plan's release, were designated in the plan as expendable, "Built prior to 1915, not fireproof, not modernized. These factors are considered as militating against its performance." None of the buildings in the proposed Seaport district was tagged for either short-term or long-term life expectancy. The plan suggested razing of the entire district so that a residential cluster to house approximately 10,000 new residents could be built.[268]

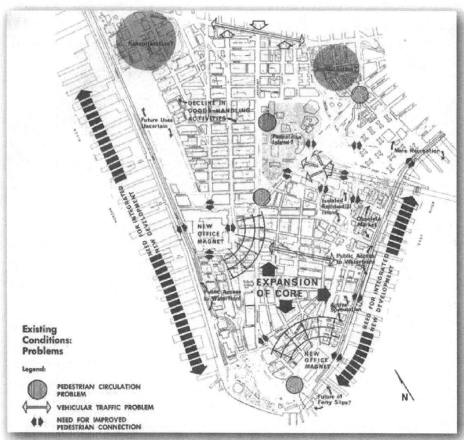

From *The Lower Manhattan Plan of 1966*, "Existing Conditions: Problems."
This diagram illustrates suggested land use and expansion plans in the
area surrounding the financial district. The South Street district is shown
at the middle right, in the area marked "Obsolete Market."[269]

A careful reading of the report reveals that these urban planners were not
averse to the *idea* of the area's maritime heritage, once the old Fulton Fish
Market moved to Hunts Point in the Bronx and cleared way for the new residential development. Despite its emphasis on commercial development and
economic revitalization, local heritage and civic memory were incorporated

into the Lower Manhattan Plan's vision for a new urban landscape. Waterfront access and recreational usage, along with a revitalized maritime-inspired district displaying "drying nets and other maritime paraphernalia, and seafood sold from permanently-anchored fishing boats" would offer a distinct reference to the memory of the old seaport's role in lower Manhattan. The plan proposed that the new residential cluster at Fulton Street might retain some links to the area's seafaring past through oyster bar cafes and "oysters sold from boats." While the plan called for removal of the seaport's outdated structures, its designers recognized the benefits of incorporating the old seaport's special character and sense of place into the new construction.[270]

The Lower Manhattan Plan's philosophy on land-use echoes earlier reports by the RPA, with its proposals for altered traffic patterns, the designation of specific "functional areas," and waterfront redevelopment. The City Planning Commission hailed the plan as "a bold guideline for the downtown renaissance;" planners and architects praised the plan as raising the bar on the aesthetics and functionality of urban redevelopment.[271] The plan had the support from key stakeholders in City government from its outset; the impact felt by the economic slump in lower Manhattan cannot be overstated. With declining employment statistics, a surplus of unoccupied office space and increasing competition with Midtown for commercial investment, lower Manhattan was seeking salvation. The area required a physical overhaul in order to attract new investors and increase the financial district's impact not only on New York City, but on the entire country. Warren Lindquist, David Rockefeller's aide and fellow D-LMA member, stated what members of the financial community most certainly felt – that lower Manhattan was "the heart pump of the capital blood that sustains the free world." Further, Lindquist felt it was the responsibility of the D-LMA to ensure that the financial community of lower Manhattan remain active in the commercial growth of not only the city, but of the nation and of the entire world.[272] The Lower Manhattan Plan was meant to reposition the city's financial district as the epicenter of capitalism and promote a new vision of modernity in urban planning. Less awe-inspiring but by no means incidental, city officials foresaw job creation and increased investment as much-needed boons to the local economy.

HISTORIC PRESERVATION AND MEMORY

The process of historic preservation is intimately tied to memory. However the influence of collective memory on urban development, while experiencing a resurgence during the 1960s, was not new to urban discourse at this time. The debate surrounding historic preservation and its implications on property rights can be traced to the pre-Civil War era, when America was very much preoccupied with nation building, westward expansion and Manifest Destiny. From the nation's earliest forays to all-points west, the acquisition, refurbishment, and resale of private property has taken precedence over any meager public interest in preservation.[273] However, by the later half of the nineteenth century, the conflict and contention wrought by the Civil War caused many Americans during that time to look nostalgically to the past, to a mythical simpler time of the colonial period. During this time of significant cultural upheavals associated with Civil War, increasing industrialization, immigration, and urbanization, the colonial past achieved an air of nostalgia.[274] Growing anxieties created by the restructuring of society manifested in a sentimental yearning for a collective memory that was itself a myth; an idealized conception of the past born from present-day anxieties about the changing political, economic and social landscape emerged. Early twentieth century Progressive Era reformists felt this yearning as well, as increased industrialization, immigration and the new social problems associated with an increasingly urbanized American society prompted a desire to incorporate vestiges of the physical past in the city's modern push forward.

Fast-forward to New York City, circa 1960, which experienced new anxieties fueled by urban renewal's swift and sweeping changes to the physical landscape, Cold War fears and the transition to a postindustrial economy. Upheavals - quite literally, city blocks were demolished, turned over, and created anew - and the fear of an uncertain future created an environment in which feelings of nostalgia and the desire to preserve if not re-create memories of the past were intensified. In the midst of urban renewal's utter chaos, the historic preservation movement functioned as a remedy to the swift pace of modernity and an appreciation for the smaller-scale of the nineteenth century cityscape. Nostalgia, however, is not the only motivating factor behind the push for historic preservation. Historic sites serve as narratives of the toil on which early industry was founded. These sites honor the enterprise and physical labor of men and women who quite literally laid the foundation for the industrializing nation, and the results of historic preservation and commemoration help create collective memories tied to place.[275]

Peter Stanford's early writings on the South Street Seaport Museum, in which he outlined his plans for the function and future of the museum district, evoke these same psychological and sociological implications of historic preservation. According to Stanford's vision, the Museum would encompass a working community of tradesmen, shops, and ship restoration activities, each contributing to the maritime ambience of the seaport's nineteenth century past. Stanford indicated the impact this new historic district might have on the city's collective memory, assuring the public that even though the forest of masts were gone from the piers at South Street, their ghosts had left the city with proud memories.[276] The South Street Seaport Museum's determination to interpret the lives of ordinary men and women of the Age of Sail signaled a shift away from the traditional canon of the history of Great Men – the history portrayed in McKay's study on South Street, for example, and the history interpreted in the Long Room at Fraunces Tavern – towards an appreciation for the vernacular history of ordinary folk who toiled and labored in a place that was first a seaport, and then a town.[277]

The community of citizens and organizations concerned with the expanding disaster zone that had transformed lower Manhattan had several key supporters, including the Landmarks Preservation Commission and the Municipal Art Society. In 1965, Mayor Wagner established the New York City Landmarks Preservation Commission and signed the city's first Landmarks Preservation Act.[278] Several local organizations were in opposition to the LPA, including the Real Estate Board of New York, the Commerce and Industry Association of New York, and the Downtown-Lower Manhattan Association. A spokesman for the D-LMA had requested the Mayor reject the bill, telling the *New York Times* that it was "complex, ambiguous in many respects and will certainly be difficult for a property owner to understand."[279] Under the new law, a landmark was defined as a structure at least thirty years old, with historical and/or architectural significance to the city. The power of the commission was less in its ability to prevent an owner from demolishing his landmark property if he was intent on doing so, but rather to delay him, whereby an agreement could be reached for rehabilitation or renovation. Many owners were far from pleased with the landmark status that was bestowed upon their properties and cited infringement of personal property rights as well as the inability to make the most optimal use of these properties. To this, however, Municipal Art Society member Arthur C. Holden replied in the *Times*, "To say they can do nothing unless they destroy a building is a palpable confession of impotence and intellectual bankruptcy."[280]

The Municipal Art Society, a local preservationist group formed in 1892, appealed to the Landmarks Preservation Commission in calling for historic landmark designation of the Schermerhorn Row buildings on Fulton Street. An active voice in preservation efforts long before the Commission was created to address these issues, the MAS had cautioned its citizens to keep diligent watch for any and all developments related to the aesthetic and architectural nature of the city, and to raise up in collective voice should developments emerge that might threaten the city's remaining links with its past.[281] Several members of the Municipal Art Society, including Ada Louise Huxtable, were resolute about the necessity for adaptive re-use of the city's many historic structures. These supporters encouraged architects to look at new ways to utilize city landmarks, including the old Merchant's House and the Astor Library, because "you can't make a museum out of every landmark."[282] Landmark designation alone was not enough to save a structure from demolition or obsolescence; in order to keep these buildings viable and integrated within the fabric of the modern city, contemporary use and economic feasibility must be prime considerations. Stanford and Friends' plans for a multi-use commercial and residential mélange at the Seaport - in addition to the proposed Maritime Museum and ship restoration activities - envisioned the adaptive reuse of Schermerhorn Row and the surrounding buildings.

A feasibility study conducted by the New York State Historical Commission provided validation for the Seaport project, outside of its architectural merits as some of the finest remaining Federalist-style structures in the city. Arguing "adaptive usage of Schermerhorn Row is not only a feasible but also a most effective solution" to the question of land use in the district, the Commission cited recent preservation ventures in the redevelopment of Georgetown, District of Columbia and Newburyport, Massachusetts.[283] The report invoked Walt Whitman's reference to New York as the *City of Ships,* in this way recalling the glory of the city's maritime history and recommending that collective memory and local heritage play "one small part" in the redevelopment of one of the world's greatest cities. Most importantly, the report insisted Schermerhorn Row represented a "visible symbol of memory," critical in maintaining the public's sense of local and national heritage.[284]

As architecture critic for the *New York Times,* Pulitzer Prize-winning Huxtable provided readers with an often scathing commentary on the loss created by urban renewal's demands for orderly progression. Huxtable chronicled the bulldozer's progression across the island of Manhattan as if she were tracking General Sherman's March to the Sea. The *Times'* critic, credited for bringing the cultural impact of architecture into the public dialogue, reported that "the southern tip of Manhattan, the city's most famous face, looks like a disaster area," argued that the city had spent twenty years "of ruthless and indiscriminate bulldozing of Manhattan's most historic areas carried out with a single-minded insensitivity compounded about equally of bureaucracy and ignorance," and remarked that "it usually takes bomb damage or bulldozer public renewal to produce clearance and rebuilding on a comparable scale." Huxtable was adroit at exposing the simple fact of economics in the urban renewal versus historic preservation game, challenging capitalism's demand for the productive use of land with her indictment, "The reasons [for demolition] are obvious. There are no profits in preservation."[285]

COMPETING VISIONS OF ROOTS AND PRIDE

A healthy, wholesome life like this in the open air, beneath a limitless expanse of sky and flying clouds, the eventful journey

*homeward, at dusk, along great stretches of quay, rich in
ever-changing scene and incident, must be its own reward.*[286]

— *CHARLES HENRY WHITE (1905)*

The South Street Seaport Museum and the Fraunces Tavern museum block project were in the company of two smaller maritime-themed commemorative projects in lower Manhattan. Plans for a maritime museum in the old U.S. Customs House on Bowling Green had been proposed a few years previously. An article in the *New York Journal American* reports on the proposed use of the old Customs House as a maritime museum, once federal offices relocated to the World Trade Center. The site housed the original Fort Amsterdam, erected in 1626, and later welcomed the U.S. Government House in 1790, built for President George Washington and mere steps from Samuel Fraunces' Tavern. Following the relocation of the federal government to Philadelphia, the site became the home of the U.S. Customs House in 1800. The current Cass Gilbert design, built in 1907, represents a glorious example of the Progressive Era's City Beautiful movement and its Beaux-Arts architecture, in which the building's aesthetic beauty matched the supremacy of the city's commercial and financial success. Reginald Marsh's painted murals upon the interior gilded rotunda are steeped in maritime lore and reflect the city's – and the nation's – maritime roots.

Although the U.S. Customs House received historic landmark designation status in 1966 as Federal Hall National Memorial, the future use of the site remained unclear. Plans for a maritime museum represented a civic project to commemorate the city's maritime history and protect whatever remained of the area's seafaring past before the urban renewal wrecking ball destroyed any last vestiges. When Peter Stanford and the Friends of South Street got down to the business of raising support – both human and financial – for the South Street Seaport Museum, Jeff Rogers of Columbia Lines informed Stanford that his team had already been working for many years to establish a maritime museum in the city's magnificent Custom's House.[287] However, with support rapidly amassing for the South Street Seaport project, plans for the U.S. Custom's House maritime museum disintegrated. Further, the Seaman's Church Institute, that sailor-friendly organization founded in 1834 and provider of bed, board, and general welfare to sailors moving in and out of port, scrapped its own plans for a maritime museum by 1967, owing to "other well-known plans for redevelopment of lower Manhattan include a maritime museum."[288]

Lower Manhattan, home of the financial district, could not support multiple maritime commemorative projects and yet all of these visions – from South Street to Fraunces Tavern to the U.S. Customs House to the Seaman's Church Institute – sprung from an appreciation for the city's earliest days as a port city, where the entire southern tip of Manhattan came alive with the smell of sea salt, the low bellow of steam whistles, and the constant churning of the harbor as tug boats and merchant ships navigated the waters in a highly complex water-ballet in which the thrill of commerce was simply invigorating. The activity of this harbor and this seaport gave birth to New York, gave birth to the nation. And while the Seaport plan meant to bring much-needed commercial activity downtown, any economic revitalization the Museum might encourage was not truly the point of the endeavor. "The real point" of the Seaport plan, said trustee Harold Logan, was to bring back something essential to the collective identity of the city, the nation, the people of the 1960s: a sense of *roots and pride*. This, said Logan, was needed "now, more than ever before."[289]

With ideological and promissory financial support from both the City and the Downtown-Lower Manhattan Association, the Fraunces Tavern museum block project remained the most ominous hurdle to the Seaport plan. Raising the necessary funds to undertake each project individually was a hefty toll; the success of simultaneous commemorative projects would tap even the deepest pockets of New York City's most philanthropic citizens. The city would not support two museum blocks mere steps from one another, no matter how great the need for heroic memory or a collective identity boost. John Pell, "scion on a Revolutionary War family" and Chairman of the Historic Sites Committee, warned Stanford he had a tough road ahead in trying to win over the support of David Rockefeller and, therefore, the downtown financial community, whose own heroes were located not in the brawny sea captains of South Street, but in the leaders of the American Revolution.[290] Memory and identity, like everything else in Gotham, comes with a price tag, and a hero is a very personal thing. The consensus among preservationists lies in the *process* of revitalizing memories of heroism and strength, not in the particular individuals or campaigns designated for interpretation.

While plans for the Fraunces Tavern museum block and the South Street Seaport Museum both sought to commemorate American heroes of an earlier age, men of bravery and dignity and noble determination who represented a time when we were good, the brute fact remained clear: the acquisition and reconstruction of memory on pricey Manhattan real estate required sound financial support.

The D-LMA felt this growing rivalry emerging along South Street and questioned the financial feasibility of the Fraunces Tavern project in light of Governor Rockefeller's approval of Seymour's maritime legislation. In a memo from Warren Lindquist to David Rockefeller in July 1966, Lindquist acknowledges fundraising for the Fraunces Tavern museum block would be "obviously and completely impossible" with viable competition at South Street.[291] The Downtown Museum of the City of New York also felt the inevitable financial pinch that would result from two similar museum block projects competing for philanthropic support downtown. Even as the Fraunces Tavern museum block project received strong support in the summer of 1966 from the Borough President of Manhattan, the City Planning Commission, the Landmarks Preservation Commission, Community Planning Board Number One, the Downtown Museum of the City of New York, the Park Department, and the Downtown-Lower Manhattan Association, the Office of the Borough President noted if the South Street project moved forward with its own plans for a state maritime museum, it would be "unlikely" that the Museum of the City of New York would remain interested in moving its maritime collections to the newly formed Downtown MCNY. Complicating the forward momentum of the Fraunces Tavern project, in December 1966 the D-LMA scrapped plans to move the four Atlas-McGrath properties from Whitehall and Front Streets to the Fraunces Tavern block, citing the structural impossibility of moving the houses intact.

In early 1967, the Downtown Museum of the City of New York was dissolved, due to lack of financial support from both public and private sources. While the City had earmarked capital and annual funds for the Fraunces Tavern project, this agreement required matching funds from private and foundational sources. With the South Street Seaport project moving full steam ahead, the D-LMA did not feel it would be possible to raise these necessary matching funds in light of competition at South Street. Warren Lindquist acknowledged "the unfortunate impact of the proposed South Street Maritime Museum project on the Fraunces Tavern project from the standpoint of duplicating in a largely identical historical field of interest."[292] When both the Fraunces Tavern and South Street Seaport Museum projects applied to the New York State Historical Trust for funding in 1967, Chairman John Pell advised the Fraunces project be downsized considerably, to include just the property of the Tavern itself and the other properties currently owned by the Sons of the Revolution. Citing the considerable increase in land values since the plan was originally proposed, the museum block project did not, in Pell's opinion, appear financially feasible. Land values on the Schermerhorn Row block at South Street, however, remained less pricey, and might be developed with better success.[293]

THE SOUTH STREET SEAPORT MUSEUM EMERGES

The South Street Seaport Museum officially opened on May 22, 1967, National Maritime Day. Pete Seeger, controversial figure of the American folk music scene, was an early Friend of the Seaport. Currently building his own replica of a nineteenth century river sloop, Seeger performed an outdoor concert at the newly opened South Street Seaport during the summer of 1967. Active in the radical anti-war movement, Seeger had joined over 100,000 protesters in an April anti-war march from Central Park to the United Nations building. The demonstration was led by anti-war activist and child rearing specialist Dr. Benjamin Spock, the Black Panthers' Stokely Carmichael, and Dr. Martin Luther King, Jr. During that demonstration, Seeger sang folksongs from atop a parade float. The *New York*

Times reported that men burned their draft cards in Central Park, protestors marched with Vietcong flags, and at least one American flag was burned. There were no such radical displays at this Seeger appearance however, and in his memoir, Stanford recalls three thousand people turning out to sing along with Seeger's songs of "protest and liberation" along the East River piers. This radical voice of the great American Folk Revival had become a good friend of South Street.

After two years of maneuverings from both the Friends of South Street and city planners, negotiations over the proposed development of South Street as a historic museum district finally simmered. By December 1968, several key developments had taken place. First, the Lower Manhattan Plan had been approved by the City Planning Commission and had been hailed by city officials, commercial developers, the Downtown-Lower Manhattan Association, and the press as a promising lifeline for the still flagging downtown economy. Second, Mayor Lindsay had created the Office of Lower Manhattan Development to act as an organizing agent and liaison between the city and commercial developers in order to implement the Plan. Third, Governor Nelson Rockefeller had signed Senator Seymour's proposed legislation, creating the New York State Maritime Museum, although in response to David Rockefeller and the D-LMA's aggressive opposition to the legislation, Seymour had agreed, at the last minute, to omit wording of any/all public funding for the Museum. The D-LMA at last conceded, "Since plans for development of the South Street Seaport Museum appear to be progressing steadily with substantial financial support from private sources, there is a reasonable basis for approval of this project," and suddenly reversed its vocal two-year opposition to the Seaport plan.[294] Fourth, the South Street Seaport Museum, backed by the Friends of the Seaport and headed by Peter Stanford, had been granted a charter by the New York State Board of Regents.

Finally, the City of New York had designated the eleven-block area as a special urban renewal district within the Brooklyn Bridge Southeast Urban Renewal District, in which the Seaport Museum was named the unassisted (that is, no public funds would be spent) sponsor of that district. Under the terms of this sponsorship, the city would acquire properties under eminent domain, but the Museum would be responsible for raising funds and covering all acquisition costs of those properties. As in the case of the New York State Maritime Museum, the charter was granted by the state, but in neither case would public funds be directed towards the cultural organizations.

Amidst critics' charges that the historic district would detract significantly from the Lower Manhattan Plan's strategy for physical and commercial revitalization of the financial district, Stanford conceptualized a multi-use commercial and residential environment at South Street. Inspired by the maritime preservation work in San Francisco and Mystic, Connecticut, Stanford envisioned a working community with restored nineteenth century row houses occupied by a mélange of house museums, cafes, small shops and exhibitions. The *neighborhood* would be the museum, "a place where citizens could seek out and enjoy an important chapter of the heritage of their city."[295] Echoing Jane Jacobs, who observed that local residents and visitors are more likely to spend time on the streets when there is a mixed-use of shops, restaurants, commercial establishments, and upper-floor offices, the Museum's earliest plans called for a lively street culture. "To keep the streets naturally alive is the essence of the restoration…Real commerce and small shops and craft activities should do much to maintain this kind of life in twentieth century terms."[296] Stanford understood that a healthy neighborhood depends upon multi-functionality, and that the unique characteristics of the seaport district would encourage and sustain an animated street culture; indeed, commercial viability was integrated into South Street's visions from the start. These expectations were heavily based on the economic success realized by San Francisco's Ghirardelli Square waterfront restoration project earlier in the decade. Not simply concerned with historic preservation and a lively street scene, Stanford envisioned a "major economic stimulus in redevelopment."[297]

Financially, the Seaport project appeared promising. Plans to sell the Seaport's air rights to neighboring properties, as the Seaport would not build up beyond the height of its present structures, would provide real income to the organization. Neighboring developers would pay heavily for the transfer of air rights from the South Street district to their own construction projects. In addition, a large influx of lower Manhattan residents was anticipated, expected to invigorate foot traffic in the neighborhood and provide a local source of patronage and consumer-based revenue. A projected 50,000 residents would soon call the neighborhood home, based on the approved Lower Manhattan Plan's proposal for residential development along the waterfront. This influx of residents would create active pedestrian traffic and support the Seaport's shops, restaurants and public events. A second residential complex, Battery Park City, was planned for the west side of lower Manhattan, expecting to house an additional 45,000 residents and providing future foot traffic to the entire area.

After a series of delays, both political and financial, Battery Park City was finally completed in 1985, but never yielded the kind of cross-town pedestrian traffic originally anticipated. Plans for the Manhattan Landing east side residential complex, a housing development spawned from D-LMA reports and the Lower Manhattan Plan, were approved by the City Planning Board but stalled during the city's recession in the early 1970s and never got off the drawing table. This, and the City of New York's severe financial deficits across the next decade, would prove a devastating blow to the Seaport's economic strategy, as the historic district was depending upon the strong residential base the new complex would bring to the area, and would have turned the sale of the Seaport's air rights into a real financial asset.[298]

CONCLUSION

*It is obvious today that there is a tide that is running in
favor of historic preservation... There is no indication
that a saturation point in interest in the past has been
reached; indeed, the social, technological, and cultural
revolution that we are experiencing in the United States
today can lead only to an expansion of that interest.*[299]

— *New York State Historical Association (1966)*

In "The South Street Maritime Museum Proposal and The Preservation of
Schermerhorn Row in New York City," Frederick Rath Jr. and the New
York State Historical Association state what has often been left out of the
postwar-era historic preservation narrative: the effects of the cultural land-
scape- including social, technological, and political change – on the preservation and commemoration impulse of the 1960s. In seeking to humanize the
modern urban landscape and our role in it, Peter Stanford underscored the
value of understanding history, in that:

We have come to see the past not as a refuge but as a challenge... We find valuable things along the way: the pride men took in their work, and the respect that existed, as well as the danger. Can we be too advanced today to learn from all of this? Let us begin, then, to learn from ourselves, from our own experiences on this globe.[300]

One purpose of understanding history is *to better understand and criticize our present society and circumstances.* By understanding our past, we gain critical knowledge and develop perspective on the present. In a sort of collective psycho-social-analysis, a growing knowledge of history – whether through traditional academic sources, material culture and artifact studies, or by reading the historical landscape – allows us to better understand and also criticize our present society.[301] In this very basic and therapeutic way, the resurgence of historic preservation during the 1960s created a mechanism from which to better understand and analyze that social-political-cultural landscape. The community of preservationists, financiers, and civic groups working to maintain a historic cityscape and create a commemorative landscape in the midst of social, technological, and political – *not simply physical* – change, engaged the larger public in the rebirth of historic preservation at that time because folks respond to the symbolic meanings imbedded in objects of material culture and architectural styles and responded to the meaning of the waterfront on the city's collective identity.

We care about *stuff,* about artifacts and architectural styles and music and ships, because these objects symbolize our often unspoken values and ideals. The manufacture of objects reflects something about the beliefs and values of the individual who made or used them. Favored objects *mean* something to us. Therefore, when we romanticize an artifact, or the more "humane scale" of a nineteenth century sloped-roof building, or the aesthetic lines of an unfurled schooner, we are declaring our own sense of style and values to the world. Historic preservation is ultimately about the preservation of artifacts, landscapes, and modes of living as manifested through these objects. Our attachments to things are heightened during moments of crisis; likewise, a return to history is heightened during moments of cultural dislocation.

This return to history and the imagined ideals of past generations occurs most often during moments of crisis, when stakeholders from various communities seek to regain a centered world upon which political, social, and moral foundations can be built. While the socio-political-cultural crisis of the 1960s was not entirely new - indeed, the nation has been sporadically wracked with social, political, racial, and economic unrest and dissent from its earliest history – the rise of mass media in its myriad forms and ubiquity of coverage during the postwar era gave traction and fuel to voices of dissent in a manner never before seen. Mass media's role in the interpretation and representation of what, in previous generations, may have remained local and seemingly isolated events, helped to generate a *crisis of cultural authority* on a national and even global scale.

Conventional wisdom surrounding the reemergence of historic preservation in the 1960s explains the impulse to preserve the aged landscape as a reaction against the physical reconfiguration of the city. The notable works of Sharon Zukin, Suleiman Osmon, Wanda Rushing, Diane Barthel, and James Lindgren locate the preservation impulse – itself a conservative process intent on retaining elements of the past – in the context of a postwar liberal agenda reacting to the urban crisis.[302] Federal urban renewal policies in the 1940s, '50s and '60s attempted to address the myriad social and economic ills of the city with the physical razing and rebuilding of the urban landscape. These postwar liberal policies, in conjunction with the private developers who reaped financial benefits from razing "blighted" neighborhoods and building public housing projects and government centers in their place, fueled a sense of urgency amongst preservationists in the 1960s. However, by overlooking the richer and more complicated cultural landscape of the Sixties - one that exists far beyond the sphere of modernist urban planning, the urban renewal bulldozer, and the political alliances that facilitated these transformations – conventional wisdom omits a critical factor in the narrative of historic preservation at that time. While the urban crisis brewed in the 1960s, and while the bulldozer and wrecking ball threatened to eradicate remaining vestiges of the nineteenth century cityscape, the question for many Americans was not simply *what is wrong with our cities?*

but fundamentally, *what is wrong with American society? What sort of people are we, we Americans?*

Historians have uncovered a search, among a certain educated and affluent demographic, for *authenticity* in the postwar and postindustrial urban landscape. This nostalgic impulse is generally understood as a response to the vanishing physical landscape of the historic city and the effect this has on urban sociability.[303] Rising real estate prices and the search for more affordable and charming neighborhoods, a desire to escape the monotony of modernist urban and suburban planning, and dissatisfaction with political machines and their partners in private redevelopment add nuance to the conventional wisdom that explains postwar preservation as an amelioration to urban renewal in the age of the urban crisis. And yet the urban crisis - culminating in summer riots blazing through the nation's urban core in 1967 and '68, flophouses of hippie youth from Haight-Ashbury to Tompkins Square Park, antiwar protests in Central Park, student takeovers at Berkeley and Columbia, draft card burnings at Whitehall Street, and proliferating protests against the nation's racial, financial and political hierarchies across the country- indicate the crisis of the 1960s was much broader than simply one of urban crime rates and deindustrialization. This larger cultural landscape of the Sixties, its ubiquitous challenges to the political, financial, racial, and moral foundations of the country, gave birth to an *anguished scrutiny* surrounding the meaning of the most fundamental tenets of American society.

We know that a search for origins is most prevalent in times of chaos. The instability of the American cultural landscape in the 1960s demanded answers to the question: *what sort of people are we, we Americans?* For many, the answer to this question might be found in the preservation and commemoration of American origin stories, of myths, of a time when we were – in hindsight, at least - good.

The trajectory of historic preservation in America dates to the late nineteenth century, its roots located in the social reform movement of the Progressive Era. We cannot look at the preservation impulse in isolation, but rather must understand its origins as part of a larger concern with social reform and as a response to change in the social landscape. In the turbulent waters of change, we keep our bearings by clinging to that which we know. "Horror at upheaval" and a disturbing sense of "technophobic gloom" combine to create a collective anxiety which renders *the past* especially comforting.[304] This renewed concern for preservation constitutes a sign of cultural crisis, a canary in a coalmine. Social reformers' concerns for the social, educational, religious, and physical well being of urban dwellers were part of the matrix in which the historic preservation flourished during the Progressive Era. Historian Randall Mason characterizes the preservation impulse at the turn of the century as a product of that era's cultural tensions, in which Progressive Era reformists responded to the cultural turbulence wrought by urban conflicts, and understood the power of collective memory in guiding the city forward.[305]

Seeking to expand our understanding of the historic preservation movement beyond the traditional bounds of *urbanism*, Page and Mason offer an important edict for analysis of the preservation impulse since the Progressive Era. That is, we must *release* the historic preservation movement from its relegation as simply a process associated with urbanism and urbanization.[306] While historic preservation in the postwar era has been primarily explored as a response to urban development, we must instead read the preservation impulse of the 1960s as a sign of the larger cultural crisis of that decade. A crisis which has been described in all manner of urgency, Technicolor, confusion, amusement, and literary gusto. From fire hoses in Birmingham, to the summer "riot seasons," to violent attacks against antiwar and student protestors, to the *hippie invasion*, to the moral ambiguity of the nation's military presence in Vietnam, to cultural alienation, to Black Power, to the assassinations of national leaders at home and the bombing of women and children abroad… crises were everywhere. "Everybody felt it."

How and why New York's old maritime district, the South Street Seaport, became an iconic symbol of roots and pride during this age of dissent developed from a confluence of wider artistic interest in New York's waterfront. Joseph Mitchell had been writing on the waterfront and the bottom of the harbor since the 1930s, his essays well known to New York literary audiences who might later help fund the South Street Seaport Museum. Malcolm Johnson's Pulitzer Prize winning expose "On the Waterfront" captivated New

Yorkers when it ran in *The New York Sun* in late 1949; the drama had become a hugely popular Academy Award winning movie starring Marlon Brando just five years later. With Manhattan's West Side piers now the hotbed of shipping activity at the Port of New York, the aging East River waterfront was all that remained of the city's preindustrial maritime past. When Senator Seymour, Peter Stanford, and the Friends of South Street showed a personal interest in resuscitating the South Street Seaport district so that the city's – the nation's – maritime roots might teach a thing or two about a slower pace of life during a time of urban unrest, they were tapping in to a much broader dissatisfaction with the existing cultural landscape. Historic preservation and heritage commemoration thus became a mechanism of amelioration and re-education during a time of cultural crisis. Alarm at the physical transformation of the city in the age of urban renewal is perhaps the most obvious explanation for the rise of urban historic preservation in the 1960s, but this concern was a symptom of a larger concern with the present crisis of fracturing and transformation in all of its forms.

It is through a reflective engagement with the past where the invaluable – *and presumably more virtuous* – lessons, ideals, and challenges of history reach us in the present.[307] Joseph Conrad's 1897 farewell salute captures this nostalgic and commemorative nod for a new generation almost three-quarters of a century later, as Americans searched for roots and pride amid the divisive cultural landscape of the present.

> *Goodbye, brothers! You were a good crowd. As good a crowd as ever fisted with wild cries the beating canvas of a heavy foresail; or, tossing aloft, invisible in the night, gave back yell for yell to a westerly gale.*[308]

View of lower Manhattan through the South Street Seaport's masts of ships.
Photographed by this author, Robin Foster, 2010

AUTHOR'S NOTE

I come from a writing family. Which isn't to say that we all must write, but many of us have, and still do, and after the joy of putting our words down on paper is satisfied, we then find a way to get those words out into the world.

My grandfather started a literary magazine in the 1930s with his friend from college, and his future wife/my grandmother, who would earn her doctorate in philosophy a few years later in 1941. They named their literary baby *The Fortnightly*, set up shop in North Beach, San Francisco, and wrote in the style of literary criticism that flourished in the '30s and '40s. The Great Depression, however, reaching its lowest point, ended that literary production after just one year. My grandfather wrote, "The Depression had subdued us." *Fortnightly* or no, he kept writing. Mostly for himself and for family. He wrote.

My great aunt and great uncle started a home printing press in the Oakland Hills, just east of San Francisco, in the early 1960s. She would do diligent research and write the stories, which were for the most part histories of local significance. Some of the copies have been handed down to me from my family, some I have purchased in used bookstores across the country. He set the type and managed the printing press with one arm (he had suffered a stroke in 1962), and she carved woodcuts and linocuts for the illustrations, and learned the craft of bookbinding. In this work of true craftsmanship, the pair hand-numbered each book they had produced themselves. *Bohemians to Hippies: Waves of Rebellion; Gertrude Stein and California;* and *Books and Societies* are some of the Rather Press titles that live on my bookshelf today.

So we write, and we publish, and we share our stories with the world. I am grateful for the inspiration. And so in the spirit of the Rather Press: *This book is printed in Garamond 11 pt. font. First print edition, March 2016.*

The Little Red House
Lois Rather, illustration credit, c 1970

NOTES

INTRODUCTION

1   Italo Calvino, *Invisible Cities* (New York: Houghton Mifflin, 1974), 11

2   South Street Seaport Museum, *South Street Seaport: A plan for a vital new historic center in Lower Manhattan* (New York: South Street Seaport Museum, 1969), 1. ***Permission to quote this and all other RAC materials contained in this work courtesy of the Rockefeller Archive Center.*** Record Group Series 2: DLMA, Inc. Series 2.5: Reports and Studies.

3   South Street Seaport Museum, *South Street Seaport*, 1

4   Peter & Norma Stanford, *A Dream of Tall Ships: How New Yorkers came together to save the city's sailing-ship waterfront* (Peekskill: Sea History Press, 2013), xxvi. Here is an invaluable account of the Seaport Museum's earliest days and it's growth during Stanford's tenure.

5   Peter & Norma Stanford, *A Dream of Tall Ships: How New Yorkers came together to save the city's sailing-ship waterfront* (Peekskill: Sea History Press, 2013), 443

6   Stanford, *A Dream of Tall Ships,* p. xxvi, xx, 318, 346, 443

7   Ibid, 330, 45, 416, 447. Stanford recalls, it was at sea where "one could deal with honest realities and learn to make one's way by man's God-given gift to learn life's truths."

8   Ibid, 147

9   Stanford, 48, 278, 189, 277. "We were working to achieve something valuable while we continued to protest the war we each opposed."

10   Jon Teaford, *The Metropolitan Revolution; The Rise of Post-Urban America* (New York: Columbia University Press, 2006), 134

11   Peter and Norma Stanford, "The Road to South Street," Alfred Stanford, *Pleasures of Sailing*, 13-14

12   Sharon Zukin. *Naked City; The Death and Life of Authentic Urban Places* (Oxford: Oxford University Press, 2010), 11

13   Robert O. Self and Thomas J. Sugrue, "The Power of Place: Race, Political Economy, and Identity in the Postwar Metropolis," in *A Companion To Post-1945 America,* Jean-Christophe Agnew & Roy Rosenzweig, eds. (Malden, MA: Blackwell Publishing, 2006), 26

14   Suleiman Osman, *The Invention of Brownstone Brooklyn; Gentrification and the Search for Authenticity in Postwar New York* (New York: Oxford University Press, 2011), 5, 11, 12

15   Ibid, 9-10

16   Wanda Rushing, *Memphis and the Paradox of Place; Globalization in the American South* (Chapel Hill: University North Carolina Press, 2009), 66-67

17   Ibid, 11

18   Teaford, *The Metropolitan Revolution,* 126

19   "Can the Big Cities Ever Come Back?" *US News World Report,* Sept. 4, 1967, p. 28, 31

20   Alison Isenberg, *Downtown America: A history of the place and the people who made it* (Chicago: University of Chicago Press, 2004) 272, 257

21   Boyer, 377

22   D.W. Meinig, "The Beholding Eye" in *Interpretation of Ordinary Landscapes,* (New York: Oxford University Press, 1979), 34

23   Susan Sontag, "Thirty Years Later," *The Three Penny Review* (Summer 1996)

24   Maurice Isserman & Michael Kazin, *America Divided: The Civil War of the 1960s* (New York: Oxford University Press, 2000), ix, 4-5. Italics added.

25   David Farber, ed. *The Sixties; From Memory to History* (Chapel Hill: University of North Carolina Press, 1994), loc 94 of 7563. Kindle edition

26   Kenneth Cmiel, "The Politics of Ci
vility, in Farber's *The Sixties,* loc 5694 of 7563; Cmiel, in Farber's *The Sixties,* loc 5736 of 7563; Chester J. Pach, Jr. "And That's the Way it Was; The Vietnam War on the Network Nightly News" in Farber's *The Sixties,* loc 1960 of 7563

27   Mary Sheila McMahon, "The American State and the Vietnam War," in Farber's *The Sixties,* loc 987-988 of 7563. George Lipsitz, "Who'll Stop the Rain? Youth Culture Rock n Roll, and Social Crises," in Farber's *The Sixties,* loc 4470 of 7563

28   Charles Kaiser, *1968 In America; Music, Politics, Chaos, Counterculture, and the Shaping of a Generation* (New York: Grover

Press, 1997), xv. "The 1960s and the 1930s were the only modern decades in which large numbers of Americans wondered out loud whether their county might disintegrate."

29   Read for example: Arthur M. Schlesinger, Jr. "America 1968: The Politics of Violence," *Harper's* Aug. 1968; any issue of *The Atlantic Monthly, Harper's Weekly, TIME* magazine, *LIFE* magazine; *The CBS Evening News With Walter Cronkite;* Paul Goodman, *Growing Up Absurd* (New York: Vintage Books, 1959); Theodore Roszak, *The Making of a Counter Culture: Reflections of the Technocratic Society and Its Youth* (1969); Tom Wolfe, *The Electric Kool-Aid Acid Test* (New York: Bantam Books, 1968); anything by Hunter S. Thompson; Judith Clavir & Stewart Edward Albert, *The Sixties Papers: Documents of a Rebellious Decade* (New York: Praeger Special Studies, 1984); Todd Gitlin, *The Sixties: Years of Hope, Days of Rage* (New York: Bantam Books, 1987); Bob Dylan, "The Times They Are A'Changin," 1963; Joni Mitchell, "Woodstock," 1969; Paul Simon, "Mrs. Robinson," 1967; Steven Stills, "For What It's Worth," 1966.

30   Os Guinness, *The American Hour; A Time of Reckoning and the Once and Future Role of Faith* (New York: The Free Press, 1993), 27-28

31   Lears, Jackson, *No Place of Grace* (Chicago: University of Chicago Press, 1981)

32   Jules David Prown, "The Truth of Material Culture: History or Fiction?" in Steven Lubar, W. David Kingery, eds. *History from Things; Essays on Material Culture* (Washington D.C.: Smithsonian Institution Press, 1993) 1, 4

33   Leslie Fielder, *The Art of the Essay* (New York: Crowell Publishers, 1958), 259

34   Robert Cantwell, *When We Were Good; The Folk Revival* (Cambridge: Harvard University Press, 1997), 15

35   Richard McKay, *South Street; A Maritime History of New York* (New York: G.P. Putnamn's Sons, 1934), 123

CHAPTER 1

36   Freidrich Schiller, "Letter VI; Letters Upon the Aesthetical Education of Man," in *Essays Aesthetical and Philosophical* (London, 1910), 37-44

37   Leo Marx, *The Machine in the Garden; Technology and the Pastoral Ideal in America* (Oxford: Oxford University Press, 1964), 370

38   Cook & Glickman, 10

39   John Lark Bryant, "A Usable Pastoralism; Leo Marx's Method in The Machine in the Garden," *American Studies*, Vol 16 No 1 (spring 1975), 63

40   Bryant, 64-65

41   Jeffrey L. Meikle, "Leo Marx's *The Machine in the Garden*," *Technology and Culture*, Vol 44 No 1 (Jan, 2003), 152

42   Meikle, 153

43   Marx, 27, 29

44   Thomas Bender, *Toward an Urban Vision*, 162

45   Thomas Roderick Dew, *The Southern Literary Messenger,* 1836

46   Lears, xi

47   xlviiIbid, 7, xvi

48   Ibid 26, 5

49   Ibid, 28

50   Ibid, 31-32

51   Lears, 60-61

52   Daniel Rodgers, *Atlantic Crossings: Social Politics in a Progressive Age* (Cambridge, MA: Belknap Press, 1998); Thomas Bender, *Nation Among Nations; America's Place in World History* (New York: Hill and Wang, 2006)

53   On the paradox of the city and reactions to modernity and urban change, see Daniel Rogers, *Atlantic Crossings*; Thomas Bender, *The Unfinished City; New York and the Metropolitan Idea* and *A Nation Among Nations; America's Place in World History*; Michael McGreer, *A Fierce Discontent; The Rise and Fall of the Progressive Movement in America;* Davarian Baldwin, *Chicago's New Negroes; Modernity, the Great Migration, and Black Urban Life*; Allen Scott & Edward Soja, *The City: Los Angeles and Urban Theory at the End of the Twentieth Century.* On literary representations of the urban experience, see Carlo Rotella, *October Cities; The Redevelopment of Urban Literature*; Thomas Heise, *Urban Underworlds; a Geography of Twentieth Century American Literature and Culture.*

54   Thomas Bender, *The Unfinished City; New York and the Metropolitan Idea* (New York: New York University Press, 2002), 104

55   Richard Lehan. *The City in Literature: an Intellectual and Cultural History* (Berkeley, University of California Press, 1998), 199

56   Heather Campbell Coyle and Joyce K. Schiller, *John Sloan's New York* (New Haven: Yale University Press, 2007), 90-92

57   Leonard Quart, "Woody Allen's New York," in *The Films of Woody Allen; Critical Essays*, Charles L.P. Silet, ed. (Lanham, MD: Scarecrow Press, Inc., 2006), 14, 19-20

58   Philip Kasinitz, ed. *Metropolis; Center and Symbol of Our Times* (New York: New York University Press, 1995), 87

59   Henry Miller, *The Air-Conditioned Nightmare* (New York: New Directions Books, 1945), 11,12

60   Miller, 13, 20. Italics added

61   Miller, 27, 30

62   Ibid, 36, 24

63   E.B. White, *Here is New York* (New York City: The Little Bookroom, 1949, 1999), 52, 22

64   Lewis Mumford, *The Culture of Cities* (New York: Harcourt, Brace and Company, Inc., 1938)

65   Lewis Mumford, *Technics and Civilization* (Chicago: University of Chicago Press, 1962), 4, 286

66   Mumford, *Technics and Civilization*, 4, 286

67   Ibid, 289, 295

68   Marx, 8-9

69   Mumford, *Technics and Civilization,* 299

70   Mumford, *Technics and Civilization*, 314. "We must, in fact, ask ourselves if the probable destination of this system is compatible with the further development of specifically human potentialities."

71   Italo Calvino, *Invisible Cities* (New York: Harcourt, Inc. 1974), 31

72   Calvino, 30

73   Mihaly Csikszentmihalyi, "Why We Need Things," from Steven Lubar and W. David Kingery, eds, *History From Things: Essays on Material Culture* (Washington D. C.: Smithsonian Institution Press, 1993), 27

74   Alain de Botton, *The Architecture of Happiness* (New York: Vintage International, 2006), 13

75   de Botton, 88

76   Ibid, 150

77   Karal Ann Marling, *George Washington Slept Here: Colonial Revivals and American Culture, 1876-1986* (Cambridge: Harvard University Press, 1988), 87. Italics added

78   Eliza Greatroix, *Old New York from the Battery to Bloomingdale* (New York: 1875)

79   William B. Rhodes, "Colonial Revival and American Nationalism." *Journal of the Society of Architectural Historians,* Vol 35 No. 4 (Dec, 1976), 239

80   Horace B. Mann, "Style in the Country House," *American Architect,* CVII (May 12, 1915), 297

81   David Gebhard, "The American Colonial Revival in the 1930s." *Winterthur Portfolio,* Vol 22, No. 2/3 (Summer-Autumn, 1987), 146

82   Gebhard, 110, 116

83   Richard Guy Wilson, *Re-creating the American Past; Essays on the Colonial Revival.* (Charlottsville: University of Virginia Press, 2006), 17, citing John D. Rockefeller Jr's "The Genesis of the Williamsburg Restoration," National Geographic, April 1937, 401

84   Rhea Talley, "The Genesis of the Williamsburg Restoration," *National Geographic,* Apr. 1937, p. 401

85   Bridget A. May, "Progressivism and the Colonial Revival: The Modern Colonial House, 1900-1920." *Winterthur Portfolio,* Vol 26 No. 2/3 (Summer-Autumn, 1991), 110. Italics added.

86   Benjamin Filene, *Romancing the Folk: Public Memory and American Roots Music.* (Chapel Hill: The University of North Carolina Press, 2000), 132

87   Filene, 10, 17, 22

88   Ibid, 22

89   Ibid, 24

90   Ibid, , 25-26

91   Ibid, 31,32,116

92   Keith Richards, *Life* (Brown, Little & Co., 2011), 109

93   W.E.B. Du Bois, *The Souls of Black Folk* (Rockville, MD: Arc Manor Publishers, 2008), 166, 169. In his poetic description of Negro "Sorrow Songs," Du Bois illustrates the link between the old spirituals to the blues, for both black and white musicians: "Through all the sorrow of the Sorrow Songs there breathes a hope – a faith in the ultimate justice of things. The minor cadences of despair change often to triumph and calm confidence. Sometimes it is faith in life, sometimes a faith in death, sometimes assurance of boundless justice in some fair world beyond. But whichever it is, the meaning is always clear: that sometime, somewhere, men will judge men by their souls and not by their skins. Is such a hope justified? Do the Sorrow Songs sing true?"

94   Cantwell, 100

95   Filene, 64-65

96   Joe Smith, *Off the Record: An Oral History of Popular Music* (New York: Warner, 1988), 13, 156

97   Richie Havens, from *They Can't Hide Us Anymore* (New York: Avon, 1999), 30

98   Ronald D. Cohen, *Rainbow Quest: The Folk Music Revival and American Society, 1940-1970* (Amherst: University of Massachusetts Press, 2002), 96

99   Ibid, 133

100   Marx, 384

101   *Time* magazine, "Man of the Year: the Inheritor," Jan 6, 1967, p.18, 23

102   To those astrologically minded, this author acknowledges that the 1960s is actually located during *the dawning* of the Age of Aquarius. For the sake of brevity, and in keeping with conventional understanding of the term, I will generally refer to the late-1960s as the Age of Aquarius, omitting the "dawning of."

CHAPTER 2

103   Arthur Schlesinger Jr. "America 1968: The Politics of Violence," *Harper's Magazine* (Aug.1968) 19

104   "The country was in a really profound state of turmoil…. The country was coming unhinged, and this was especially clear when I got back from Vietnam… Twenty-four hours after retuning from Vietnam, I was gassed as I tried to move in and around Berkeley. It was unbelievable, just mind-bending." National Endowment for the Humanities Chairman William Adams, from *Humanities*, Nov/Dec 2014, p. 11

105   Gabrielle Esperdy, "Ugly America; From the pages of Life, a complex view of the mid-century commercial landscape," *Places Journal* (Nov. 2014) https://placesjournal.org/article/ugly-america

106   William Prochnau, *Once Upon a Distant War: David Halberstam, Neil Sheehan, Peter Arnet – Young War Correspondents and Their Early Vietnam Battles* (New York: Crown Publishing, 1995), 60

107   Todd Gitlin, *The Sixties: Years of Hope, Days of Rage* (New York: Bantam Books, 1987), 343

108   Eric Goldman, "Good-by to the 'fifties - and good riddance," *Harper's,* Jan. 1960. "…We were badly scared by the Communists, so scared

that we are leery of anybody who even so much as twits our ideas, our customs, or our leaders."

109   Alexander Bloom and Wini Breines. *Takin' It To The Streets; A Sixties Reader* (New York: Oxford University Press, 2010), 5. Also see David Halberstam, *The Fifties* (Ballantine Books, 1994) for a cultural history of the decade.

110   Bloom and Breines, 5

111   Tom Wicker, "The Wrong Rubicon: LBJ and the War," *The Atlantic,* May 1968, p. 65

112   Nicholas von Hoffman, "The Class of '43 is Puzzled," *The Atlantic,* Oct 1968

113   Gitlin, 29

114   Maurice Isserman and Kazin, Michael. *America Divided: The Civil War of the 1960s* (New York: Oxford University Press, 2008), 19

115   Midge Decter, "Anti -Americanism in America," *Harper's* (April 1968), 42

116   Eric Goldman, "Goodby to The Fifties and Good Riddance," in Katharine Whittemore and Ellen Rosenbush, eds, *The Sixties: Recollections of the Decade from Harper's Magazine* (New York: Franklin Square Press, 2010), 6

117   For history of riots, rebellion, dissent and general mob-rule in America, there is extensive scholarship. To begin, see Iver Bernstein, *The New York City Draft Riots; Their Significance for American Society and Politics in the Age of the Civil War*; (Bison Books, 2010); Edwin

Burrows and Mike Wallace, *Gotham: A History of New York City to 1898* (New York: Oxford University Press, 1999); Michael Feldberg, *The Turbulent Era; Riot and Disorder in Jacksonian America* (Oxford: Oxford University Press, 1980); Paul A. Gilge, *The Road to Mobocracy* (Chapel Hill: University of North Carolina Press, 1987); Kenneth Jackson and David Dunbar, *Empire City; New York Through the Centuries* (New York: Columbia Univ Press, 2002); Michael McGerr, *A Fierce Discontent; The Rise and Fall of the Progressive Movement in America* (Oxford: Oxford University Press, 2003); Joanne Reitano, *The Restless City; A Short History of New York from Colonial Times to the Present* (New York: Routeledge, 2006); Carl Sandburg, *The Chicago Race Riots, July 1919* (Dover Books, 2013)

118 Gitlin, 83

119 Ibid, 137

120 Jason Sokol, *There Goes My Everything; White Southerners in the Age of Civil Rights, 1945-1975* (New York: Vintage Books, 2006), 6

121 Fanny Lou Hamer testimony before the Credentials Committee, Democratic National Convention. Atlantic City, New Jersey, August 22, 1964.

122 Anderson, 57

123 Anderson, 62

124 Gitlin, 4

125 Mario Savio speech on the steps of Sproul Hall, University of California Berkeley, Dec. 1964

126   Anderson, 109

127   US Senator Barry Goldwater's speech accepting the Republican Presidential Nomination

128   Persistent boos, cat-calls, and fistfights were not uncommon to the 1964 Republican National Convention, which was held at the Cow Palace in San Francisco. Gov. Nelson Rockefeller, a moderate, was almost booed off the podium. *New York Times'* reporter Anthony Lewiss found "no great mystery" in the week's animosity: "Within the Republican party, the deep conservatives who were dominant this week have long felt that they were the real majority," unhappy with the Eisenhower administration, Eastern liberals, and "sensation seeking columnists and commentators." Reporter Lewiss acknowledges this deep conservative stems from nostalgia: "a yearning for simpler, purer days when… we did not have to worry about overcrowded cities and Negroes demanding their rights and foreign countries refusing to follow the American way…. There is also a great sense of frustration about the state of the world." Anthony Lewis, "Convention Mood Reflects a Historic Change," *NYT* Jul 19, 1964.

129   *LIFE* magazine, "Plot to Behead the Statue of Liberty," Feb 26, 1965, p. 38

130   *LIFE*, "Students in a Ferment," p. 22-33

131   Paul Potter speech "March On Washington," April 17, 1965

132   Bloom and Breines, 193

133   Steven Stills, "For What It's Worth" song title, 1966

134 David Frey, Scott Davis, Stephen Stills, Ben Mcdonald, "For What It's Worth" lyrics, 1966

135 Gitlin, 243

136 Gitlin, 344

137 *LIFE,* June 10, 1966

138 Stokeley Carmichael speech, "What We Want," 1966

139 "Washington Today," *The Norwalk Hour,* Norwalk, CT, Aug 8, 1966

140 *LIFE* magazine, "Negro Revolt: the Flames Spread," Aug 4 1967, p. 16-29

141 *TIME,* "Scorecard for the Cities," Sept 13, 1968

142 Dan Wakefield, "Supernation at Peace and War," *The Atlantic,* Mar 1968

143 Vincent Cannato, "No-Fault Liberalism," *City Journal,* June 3, 2004

144 *TIME,* "Runaway Kids," Nov 3 1967, p. 18-29

145 David Farber, ed. *The Sixties; From Memory to History* (Chapel Hill: Univ of North Carolina Press, 1994), loc 56 of 7563. Kindle edition

146 Tom Wolfe, *The Electric Kool-Aid Acid Test* (New York: Bantam Books, 1968), 35

147   The *New York Times,* "Chase Bank Defends South African Loans: Companies Hold Annual Meetings," Mar 29 1967

148   D. Rockefeller, 214. RAC Library, 332.1092 ROC

149   D. Rockefeller, 214-215

150   The *New York Times*, "Students Run Columbia Protest Along Principles of Democracy," Apr 27, 1968; "Columbia Closes Campus After Disorders," Apr 25, 1968; "1000 Police Act to Oust Students," Apr 30, 1968

151   Columbia University President Grayson Kirk, statement issued on April 12, 1968

152   Mark Rudd, open letter to Grayson Kirk, April 1968

153   Tom Hayden, quoted in Norman Mailer, "Miami and Chicago" *Harpers*, Nov 68, p. 95

154   Reference to the 1961 novel by Irving Stone

155   Norman Mailer, "On the Steps of the Pentagon," *Harper's*, Mar 1968, p. 83

156   Richard Nixon speech to the Republican National Convention, Miami, August 1968

157   Reference to Joni Mitchell's song "Woodstock," 1969. "And we've got to get ourselves back to the garden."

158   Mailer, "Miami and Chicago," 100

159   Gitlin p. 333

160   Gitlin, 332

CHAPTER 3

161   Richard C. McKay, *South Street; A Maritime History of New York* (New York: G.P. Putnam's Sons, 1934), 309

162   McKay, 22

163   While on a stroll across the lower east side of Manhattan, this author quite literally stumbled upon the final resting place of said Preserved Fish at the New York City Marble Cemetery, the city's second non-sectarian burial place open to the public. Preserved Fish's final resting place is located on East 2nd Street, internment location #75. The New York City Marble Cemetery received historic designation status from the NYC Landmarks Preservation Commission in March, 1969.

164   McKay, 310

165   Reprinted in McKay, 54-55

166   McKay 90

167   Ibid, 125

168   Ibid, 172, 266

169   Ibid, 249

170   Ibid, 404, 250

171   Joanne Reitano, *The Restless City: A Short History of New York from Colonial Times to the Present* (New York: Routledge, 2010), 32

172   Sean Wilentz, *Chants Democratic: New York City and the Rise of the American Working Class* (Oxford: Oxford University Press, 2004), 286

173   Reitano, 33, 36

174   Ibid, 35

175   McKay, 207

176   Reitano, 51

177   Jeffrey Bolster, *Black Jacks: African American Seamen in the Age of Sail* (Cambridge: Harvard University Press, 1997), 176-180

178   "The Markets of New York," *Harper's New Monthly Magazine* (July 1867) 235

179   Kurlansky, 235, 197

180   Ted Steinberg, *Gotham Unbound; The Ecological History of Greater New York* (New York: Simon & Schuster, 2014), 166

181   Kurlansky, 62, 65, 102, 158, 113, 160

182   McKay, 404

183   The *New York Times*, April 22, 1870

184   George B. Post's New York Produce Exchange building, erected in 1884, was demolished in 1957 during the national wave of postwar urban renewal. The original structure, ablaze in fiery red brick, was the focal point of the nation's produce and commodities exchange, where national and global prices for commodities like wheat, corn, petroleum, and turpentine were set daily. Post went on to design the New York Stock Exchange with his firm in 1903. Christopher Gray, "A Brick Beauty Bites the Dust," The *New York Times, Aug.* 24, 2014.

185   H. Wunderlich & Co., "Work of an American Etcher; Art at Home and Abroad," The *New York Times,* July 6, 1919

186   David Lowenthal, "The Heritage Crusade and Its Contradictions," in Max Page and Randall Mason, *Giving Preservation a History* (New York: Routledge, 2004), 23

187   Randall Mason, "Historic Preservation, Public Memory, and the Making of Modern New York City" in Max Page and Randall Mason, *Giving Preservation a History* (New York: Routledge, 2004), 142

188   Randall Mason, *The Once and Future New York; Historic Preservation and the Modern City* (Minneapolis: University of Minnesota Press, 2009), 143

189   Charles Henry White, "In the Street," *Harper's*, Feb. 1905, 275

190   McKay, 416

191   Kenneth Campbell, "South Street," *The New Yorker*, Apr. 28, 1928. p. 34

192   *Sunday News Magazine*, New York, Oct 16, 1983, "Changing Scene: New York Then and Now," by Margot Gayle. **Permission to quote this and all other N-YHS materials contained in this work courtesy of the N-YHS.** Guide to the Margot Gayle Papers 1959-2005, MS 241; Box 6, Folder 24: Fraunces Tavern. 17

193   Robert J. Kelly, "The Last Waterfront: The Fulton Fish Market and the ILA as Family Businesses." In *The Upperworld and the Underworld; Criminal Justice and Public Safety* (New York: Kluwer Academic/Plenum Publishers, 1999),106. To note: The Morello Family was among the first and most powerful crime families in New York, and spawned legendary mobsters and future dons Lucky Luciano and Frank Costello. Renamed the Genovese family when Vito Genovese became Boss in the 1950s, the family still exists today.

194   James B. Jacobs, Coleen Friel, Robert Riddick, *Gotham Unbound: How New York City Was Liberated from the Grip of Organized Crime* (New York: New York University Press, 1999), 46-7

195   The *New York Times,* "Market Men Glad To Buy Protection," Jan 16, 1934

196   "Cook, Fred. Politics, Protection and Fish," *The Nation,* 480

197   Joseph Mitchell, *Up in the Old Hotel* (New York: First Vintage Books, 1938, 1993), 439

198   Mitchell, *Up in Old Hotel,* 303

199   Mitchell, 312

200   Mitchell, *My Ears Are Bent,* 245

201   Mitchell, *Up in Old Hotel*, 313

202   The *New York Times*, "Fulton Fish Market Becomes an Exchange for Products of the World," Jun 24, 1956

203   Malcolm Johnson, *On the Waterfront: The Pulitzer-Prize Winning Articles that Inspired the Classic Film and Transformed the New York Harbor* (New York: Chamberlain Bros., 2005), 3

204   Johnson, 4, 5, 9, 19

205   Ibid, 132, 3

206   Ibid, 53, 22

207   Richard Kreitner, "February 9, 1737: Thomas Paine is Born," in *The Nation* online edition, Feb. 9, 2015

208   Carl Van Doren, "Romances of Adventure," in *The American Novel* (New York: MacMillan, 1921), 73-74. Of note: Carl Van Doren is a relation of this author.

209   Van Doren, 74

210   Brodhead, 2

211   Ibid, 2,4,9

212   Alan Trachtenberg, *The Incorporation of America: Culture and Society in the Gilded Age* (New York: Hill and Wang, 1982), 201-203, 205, 225-227

213   Wai Chi Dimock, *Empire for Liberty: Melville and the Poetics of Individualism* (Princeton: Princeton University Press, 1989), 6

214   Leo Gurko, "The Heroic Impulse in 'The Old Man and the Sea'" *The English Journal,* Vol 44 No 7 (Oct 1955), 378-380

215   Mario Vargas Llosa and Thilo Ullman, "Hemingway," *Salmagundi,* No 128/129 (Fall 2000-Winter 2001), 42-44. Italics added.

216   Cain, 117, 120

217   Adams, 26

218   Hemingway, *The Old Man and The Sea* (New York: Scribner, 1951), 29-31

219   Hemingway, 106, 108

220   Leo Gurko, "The Heroic Impulse in *The Old Man and the Sea.*" *The English Journal,* Vol. 44, No. 7 (Oct, 1955), 381

221   Bernard Berenson, on *Old Man and The Sea*, reprinted in Carlos Baker, ed., *Ernest Hemingway, Selected Letters; 1917-1961* (New York: Charles Scribner's Sons, 1981), 785. Italics added.

CHAPTER 4

222   Meinig, D.W. "The Beholding Eye" in *Interpretation of Ordinary Landscapes* (New York: Oxford University Press, 1979), 34

223   Paul Simon, "Mrs. Robinson" lyric, 1967

224   Johnson, 273

225   ***An earlier version of this chapter was first published in The Journal of Urban History, Sage Publications, September 2013.*** Thank you to Sage, its reviewers and editors.

226   A shout-out to the exhibition curated by this author and Dr. Clement Price for Rutgers University-Newark, 2013: "Bricks, Mortar, Memories, and Pride: The James Street Commons Reconsidered."

227   Lindgren, James M. *Preserving South Street Seaport; The Dream and Reality of a New York Urban Renewal District* (New York: New York University Press, 2014), 32, 79

228   Lindgren, 35

229   Ibid, 54

230   Peter and Norma Stanford, *A Dream of Tall Ships; How New Yorkers came together to save the city's sailing-ship waterfront* (Peekskill: Sea History Press, 2013), 277-78

231   David Lowenthal, "Age and Artifact," in *Interpretation of Ordinary Landscapes,* (New York: Oxford Univ Press, 1979), 103

232   The *New York Times,* "Plea to Curb the Bulldozer," Oct 13, 1963, p. 80

233   Personal recollection of Whitney Seymour. New York Preservation Archive Project, interview with Whitney North Seymour Jr., by Anthony C. Wood. July 29, 2006 http://www.nypap.org/content/whitney-north-seymour-jr-oral-history-interview

234   Ada Louise Huxtable, "Landmark Plan Stirs Wall Street Controversy," *New York Times,* Dec 17, 1966

235   Western Union Telegram from Edmund F. Wagner, President of DLMA to Gov. Nelson A. Rockefeller. June 10, 1966. Rockefeller

Archive Center, Record Group IV 3B 24, D-LMA Projects South Street Seaport 1966. S 2.3, B167, F1594. Telegrams were routinely written in all capital letters.

236   Letter from John B. Goodman, D-LMA to Robert R. Douglass, Esq. Counsel to the Governor. July 18, 1966. ***Permission to quote this and all RAC materials contained in this work courtesy of the Rockefeller Archive Center.*** Record Group IV 3B 24, D-LMA Projects South Street Seaport 1966. S 2.3, B167, F1594

237   Letter from John B. Goodman, Exec VP at DLMA to Robert R. Douglass, Esq. Counsel to Gov. Rockefeller. July 18, 1966 RAC, Record Group DLMA, Series 2, Sub-series 2.3 Projects South Street Seaport 1966, Box 167 Folder 1594

238   Letter from Sylvan Lawrence Company Inc. (Real Estate) to Gov. Rockefeller. July 19, 1966. Rockefeller Archive Center, Record Group IV 3B 24, D-LMA Projects South Street Seaport 1966. S 2.3, B167, F1594

239   Personal recollection of Whitney Seymour. New York Preservation Archive Project, interview with Whitney North Seymour Jr., by Anthony C. Wood. July 29, 2006.

240   Randall Mason refers to the search for a "usable past" as a remedy for the culturally disorienting effects of urban modernization during the Progressive Era. "Historic Preservation, Public Memory, and the Making of New York City," *Giving Preservation a History*, 143

241   "Preliminary Proposal for the Development of the Fraunces Tavern Block as an Historic District," Nov. 26, 1963, James Grote Van Derpool, Executive Director of the Landmarks Pres Committee of the City of New York. Rockefeller Archive Center, DLMA Projects, Fraunces Tavern 1963-1990. p. 1-2

242   The reader is asked to recall our earlier examination of the Colonial Era revival in architecture, Chapter One, in which David Rockefeller's father, John D. Rockefeller, Jr., was the premier supporter of the Colonial Williamsburg historic preservation project in the early 1930s.

243   D. Rockefeller, *Memoirs,* p. 214-215

244   Letter from John B. Goodman, Exec VP at DLMA to Robert R. Douglass, Esq. Counsel to Gov. Rockefeller. July 18, 1966. RAC, Record Group DLMA, Series 2, Sub-series 2.3 Projects South Street Seaport 1966, Box 167 Folder 1594

245   Capital Projects Analysis, Nov 9, 1966, MCNY. RAC, DLMA Series 2.3 Projects, Landmarks. Record Group IV 3B 24, Box 112, Folder 1207; Nov 1966-Dec 1967

246   The *New York Times,* "City Aides Fight For 4 Landmarks," by Edward C. Burks, Nov. 13, 1966 (p. 66)

247   Museum of the City of New York, "Memorandum Re Downtown Museum for Discussion at the Board Meeting on October 18, 1966. Rockefeller Archive Center, Record Group DLMA Projects: Marine Museums 1959-70, Series 2.3, Box 127, Folder 1321, p. 1

248   Ada Louise Huxtable, "Lively Original U.S. Dead Copy," *NYT,* May 9, 1965. To note: John D. Rockefeller Jr. was a principal champion and funder of Colonial Williamsburg; it was John D.'s son, David Rockefeller, who now supported the Fraunces Tavern museum block project.

249   Ada Louise Huxtable, "Lively Original U.S. Dead Copy," *NYT,* May 9, 1965

250   Notes on Meeting of Tuesday July 26, 1966, Office of the Borough President of Manhattan on Proposed Downtown Museum of the City of New York. RAC, Record Group DLMA, Projects/ Landmarks, Jan – Sept 1966, p. 1-3

251   "Memorandum Re Downtown Museum for Discussion at the Board Meeting on October 18, 1966. p. 4-5

252   "Tactically Logical Cruiser," *TIME* magazine, Jan. 11, 1943, p. 52

253   James M. Lindgren, *Preserving South Street; The Dream and Reality of a New York Urban Renewal District* (New York: NYU Press, 2014), 5

254   Stanford would later describe the New York State Maritime Museum as "just another musty little museum in a corner." Peter Stanford, "We Could Do No Less then Respond with Loyalty," *Sea History* (Summer 1981), 7; Lindgren, 139 -141

255   Peter Stanford, "One Man's View of the Emergence of New York's New Sea Museum," *Curator* Vol. 13, Iss. 4 (Oct. 1970), 271

256   Stanford, *A Dream of Tall Ships*, 318."Our museum would remind people of this inspired and revived concept [the agora] and it might indeed serve as a seedbed for a revival of a more caring spirit."

257   Ibid, 19

258   *South Street Seaport Museum; A proposal to recreate the historic 'Street of Ships' as a major recreational and cultural resource in the heart of New York City*, July 1967. In the proposal, Seaport founders cite the maritime restoration successes in San Francisco, in which "over

$20 million of private capital development went into the rehabilita-. tion of the waterfront that followed the establishment of the museum and state historic park…visited by some 3 million tourists annually," 9, 18. Rockefeller Archive Center, Record Group IV 3B 24, Series 2 D-LMA, Sub-series 2.3 Projects, South Street Seaport, 1969-1972. Box 167, folder 1595

259   Letter from Peter Stanford to Warren Lindquist, Chase Manhattan Bank, Aug. 25, 1967. Rockefeller Archive Center, Record Group IV 3B 24, Series 2 D-LMA, Sub-series 2.3 Projects, South Street Seaport, 1969-1972. Box 167, folder 1595

260   Mystic Seaport is an invented 17-acre living history maritime museum on the coast of Connecticut. It was established in 1929 as a maritime historical association and served as a gauge as Stanford developed his own vision for the South Street Seaport Museum. Stanford sought greater authenticity at South Street. Mystic Seaport is indeed well-presented, and widely regarded as an expensive, family-friendly tourist destination, although critics often cite its artificial reconstruction.

261   Eric Darton, *Divided We Stand: A Biography of New York City's World Trade Center* (New York: Basic Books, 2001), 28

262   Darton, 28

263   According to the RPA report, "Some of the poorest people live in conveniently located slums on high-priced land…A stone's throw from the stock exchange, the air is filled with the aroma of roasting coffee…In the very heart of the 'commercial' city on Manhattan Island south of 59th Street, the inspectors in 1922 found nearly 420,000 workers, employed in factories. *Such a situation outrages one's sense of order. Everything seems misplaced. One yearns to*

re-arrange the hodge-podge and put things where they belong." (my italics). The fact that the RPA found the aroma of roasting coffee an insult to the potential of the financial district is, in this age of Starbucks and the $5 cup of coffee, ironic and amusing.

264   Darton, 65

265   Samuel Zipp, *Manhattan Projects: The Rise and Fall of Urban Renewal in Cold War New York* (New York: Oxford University Press, 2010), 5

266   Zipp, *Manhattan Projects,* 162

267   In her introduction to the reprint of *The Lower Manhattan Plan of 1966,* Ann Buttenweiser notes that roughly 25% of all buildings in the Wall and Broad Street areas had been razed and rebuilt during the 1920's, and that, curiously, "No remorse was expressed, however, for the loss of landmarks of the city's early skyscraper history." The reaction to the urban renewal schemes of the 1960's, then, must be viewed in the context of broader factors which characterize that era.

268   Carol Willis, ed., *The Lower Manhattan Plan: The 1966 Vision for Downtown New York* (New York: Princeton Architectural Press, 2002), 25-27

269   City Planning Commission, The Lower Manhattan Plan of 1966

270   Willis, *The Lower Manhattan Plan,* 75, 85

271   Huxtable, "City Gets Sweeping Plan for Rejuvenating Lower Manhattan," The *New York Times,* June 22, 1966

272   John H. Mollenkopf, ed. *Power, Culture and Place: Essays on New York City* (USA: Russell Sage Foundation Publications, 1988), 175

273   Boyer, 386

274   Boyer, 387

275   Diane Barthel, *Historic Preservation: Collective Memory and Historical Identity* (New Brunswick: Rutgers University Press, 1996), 154

276   Peter Stanford, *A Walk through South Street in the Afternoon of Sail* (New York: South Street Seaport Museum, 1967), inside back cover

277   Peter Stanford, "One Man's View of the Emergence of New York's New Sea Museum," *Curator; a quarterly publication of the American Museum of Natural History,* Vol 13 Iss 4 (October 1970), 281

278   By the time NYC had adopted its landmarks preservation law in 1965, it was approximately the 70th U.S. city to do so. Sherwin D. Smith, "The Great Landmark Fight," *New York Times,* Mar 27, 1966

279   Thomas Ennis, "Landmark Bill Signed by Mayor," The *New York Times,* Apr 20, 1965

280   Smith, "The Great Landmarks Fight," *New York Times,* Mar 27, 1966

281   Francis Keally, Past President of Municipal Art Society of New York, *Letters to the Times*: "Saving City's Landmarks," *New York Times,* Oct. 4, 1961. Note: Senator Seymour had briefly held the

office of President of the MAS in 1965 before he resigned that post to run for the State Senate seat to which he was ultimately elected.

282   Mark Hawthorne, "New Roles Urged for Landmarks," *New York Times,* June 20, 1965

283   *The South Street Maritime Museum Proposal and The Preservation of Schermerhorn Row in New York City; A Feasibility Study for The New York State Council on the Arts.* By Frederick L. Rath, Jr. New York State Historical Association. Cooperstown, NY. March 10, 1966. Rockefeller Archive Center, Record Group IV 3B 24, D-LMA Projects South Street Seaport 1966. S 2.3, B167, F1594. p. 12

284   *The South Street Maritime Museum Proposal...,* 12

285   Huxtable, "Downtown New York Begins to Undergo Radical Transformation," The *New York Times*, March 27, 1967; "Where Ghosts Can Be at Home," The *New York Times*, April 7, 1968; "A New City is Emerging Downtown," The *New York Times,* March 29, 1970; "Goodbye Worth Street: A New York Tragedy," The *New York Times,* Dec. 2, 1962

286   *Harper's Magazine*, "The Fulton Street Market," Charles Henry White (Sept 1905)

287   Ibid,

288   Letter from Manhattan Borough President, Community Planning Board to David Rockefeller, Chairman D-LMA, Feb. 6, 1967. RAC, Record Group DLMA Projects: Landmarks, Nov 1966-Dec 1967

289   Stanford, *A Dream of Tall Ships,* 377

290   Stanford, 105

291   Memo from Warren Lindquist to David Rockefeller, July 1, 1966. RAC, DLMA Series 2.3 Projects, Landmarks, 1965-1981. Record Group IV 3B 24, Box 112, Folder 1206; Jan-Sept 1966

292   DLMA internal memo, Dec 20, 1966. Rockefeller Archive Center, Record Group DLMA Projects: Marine Museums 1959-70, Series 2.3, Box 127, Folder 1321

293   DLMA memo from Goodman to FILES re: Fraunces Tavern and South Street Maritime Museum Projects, Sept. 18, 1967. RAC DLMA Series 2.3 Projects, Landmarks. Record Group IV 3B 24, Box 112, Folder 1207; Nov 1966-Dec 1967

294   D-LMA memo to members of the Executive and Planning Committee from John H.G. Pell, Chairman Historic Sites Committee Re: South Street Seaport Museum, May 21, 1968. D-LMA, Projects: So Street Seaport 1968, Series 2.3, Box 167, folder 1596

295   South Street Seaport Museum, *South Street Seaport: A plan,* 1

296   Ibid, 15, 19

297   Letter from Peter Stanford, Chairman Friends of the South Street Seaport
Maritime Museum to John B Goodman, D-LMA. Dec 16, 1966. Rockefeller Archive Center, Record Group IV 3B 24, D-LMA Projects South Street Seaport 1966. S 2.3, B167, F1594

298   Max Seigel, "Manhattan Landing Denounced by Three Borough Presidents," *New York Times*, June 23, 1972

CONCLUSION

299   Frederick L. Rath, Jr. & New York State Historical Association, "The South Street Maritime Museum Proposal and The Preservation of Schermerhorn Row in New York City; a Feasibility Study for the New York State Council on the Arts" (March 10, 1966) Rockefeller Archive Center, Record Group IV 3B 24, Series 2 D-LMA, Sub-series 2.3. p 12. Italics added.

300   Peter Stanford, "One Man's View of the Emergence of New York's New Sea Museum," *Curator; a quarterly publication of the American Museum of Natural History,* Vol 13 Iss 4 (October 1970), 281

301   Mark P. Leone & Barbara J. Little, "Artifacts as Expressions of Society and Culture: Subversive Genealogy and the Value of History" in Steven Lubar, W. David Kingery, eds. *History from Things; Essays on Material Culture* (Washington D.C.: Smithsonian Institution Press, 1993), 162

302   Preservation, or the verb "to preserve" means "to retain, to make lasting." The process of preservation is, quite literally, a conservative process, as "conservative" means "having the tendency to conserve or preserve."

303   Zukin, *Naked City*, x, xii, 4-5, 11; Osman, *Brownstone Brooklyn*, 5, 9-10, 12, 14

304   Max Page and Randall Mason, 23- 25

305   Mason, 237

306   Mason, xxviii

307   Max Page, *The Creative Destruction of Manhattan, 1900-1940* (Chicago: University of Chicago Press, 1999), 129. Italics added.

308   Joseph Conrad, *The Niggar of the Narcissus*, 1914

BIBLIOGRAPHY

Abbott, Berenice. *Changing New York*. New York: The New Press, 1997.

Adams, Jon Robert. "Chapter 1: The Great General Was a Has-Been; The World War II Hero in 1950s Conformist Culture," in *Male Armor; The Soldier-Hero in Contemporary American Culture* (University of Virginia Press, 2012).

Albert, Judith Clavir & Stewart Edward Albert. *The Sixties Papers: Documents of a Rebellious Decade*. New York: Praeger Special Studies, 1984.

American Institute of Architects. *Guide to New York City*. New York: Macmillian Company, 1968.

Anderson, Terry H. *The Movement and the Sixties*. New York: Oxford University Press, 1995.

The Atlantic magazine

    Wicker, Tom. "The Wrong Rubicon: LBJ and the War." May 1968.

    Von Hoffman, Nicholas. "The Class of '43 is Puzzled." Oct. 1968.

    Wakefield, Dan. "Supernation at Peace and War." Mar. 1968.

Baker, Carlos, ed., *Ernest Hemingway, Selected Letters; 1917-1961*. New York: Charles Scribner's Sons, 1981.

Barlow, Elizabeth. "On New York's aged waterfront, a pinch of salt." *Smithsonian*, Vol 2 No 5 (Aug 1971).

Barthel, Diane. *Historic Preservation: Collective Memory and Historical Identity*. New Brunswick: Rutgers University Press, 1996.

Bell, Daniel. "The Racket-Ridden Longshoremen: The Web of Economics and Politics." In *The End of Ideology*. New York: The Free Press of Glencoe, 1960.

Bender, Thomas. *Toward and Urban Vision; Ideas and Institutions in Nineteenth Century America*. Baltimore: John Hopkins University Press, 1975.

Bender, Thomas. *The Unfinished City; New York and the Metropolitan Idea*. New York: New York University Press, 2002.

Bender, Thomas. *A Nation Among Nations; America's Place in World History*.

Bennett, William James. "South Street from Maiden Lane." Aquatint, from *Megarey's Street Views in the City of New-York*, c. 1834. Collection of the NYH-S.

Bloom, Alexander and Wini Breines. *Takin' It To The Streets; A Sixties Reader*. New York: Oxford University Press, 2010.

Bolster, Jeffrey. *Black Jacks: African American Seamen in the Age of Sail*. Cambridge: Harvard University Press, 1997.

Boyer, M. Christine. "Cities for Sale." In *Variations on a theme park: the new American city and the end of public space,* Michael Sorkin. New York: Hill and Wang, 1992.

Boyer, M. Christine. *The City of Collective Memory: Its Historical Imagery and Architectural Entertainments*. Cambridge: MIT Press, 1996.

Boyes, Georgina. *The Imagined Village: Culture, Ideology, and the English Folk Revival*. New York: Manchester University Press, 1993.

Brinkley, Douglas. *Cronkite*. New York: Harper Collins Publishers, 2012. Kindle edition.

Brodhead, Richard H, ed., *New Essays on Moby-Dick; or, The Whale*. New York: Cambridge University Press, 1986.

Bryant, John Lark. "A Usuable Pastoralism; Leo Marx's Method in *The Machine in the Garden," American Studies*, Vol 16 No 1 (Spring 1975).

Buffalo Springfield, "For What It's Worth," rec. 1966.

Cain, William E. "Death Sentences: Rereading 'The Old Man and the Sea'" *The Sewanee Review*, Vol 114, No 1 (Winter, 2006).

Calvino, Italo. *Invisible Cities*. New York: Harcourt, Inc. 1974.

Campbell, Kenneth. "South Street." *The New Yorker*, Apr. 28, 1928.

Cannato, Vincent. "No-Fault Liberalism," *City Journal*, June 3, 2004.

Cantwell, Robert S. *When We Were Good: The Folk Revival*. Cambridge: Harvard University Press, 1997.

Chudacoff, Howard P. and Judith E. Smith. *The Evolution of American Urban Society, Sixth Edition*. Upper Saddle River: Pearson Prentice Hall, 2005.

Cohen, Ronald D. *Rainbow Quest: The Folk Music Revival and American Society, 1940-1970*. Amherst: University of Massachusetts Press, 2002.

Coleman, Martin A. "Emerson's 'Philosophy of the Street.'" *Transactions of the Charles S. Peirce Society*, Vol 36 No. 2 (Spring 2000).

Cook, Fred J. "Politics, Protection and Fish." *The Nation*, June 1, 1957.

Cook, James, Lawrence Glickman, Michael O'Malley, eds. "Introduction," *The Cultural Turn in US History*. University of Chicago Press, 2008.

Cowan, Michael H. *City of the West: Emerson, America, and Urban Metaphor*. New Haven: Yale University Press, 1967.

Cowie, Jefferson and Josehp Heathcott. *Beyond the Ruins: The Meanings of Deindustrialization*. IIr Press Books, 2003.

Coyle, Heather Campbell and Joyce K. Schiller. *John Sloan's New York*. New Haven: Yale University Press, 2007.

Craig-Smith, Stephen J. and Michael Fagence, ed. *Recreation and Tourism as a Catalyst for Urban Waterfront Redevelopment: an International Survey*. Westport, CT: Praeger, 1995.

Cram, Ralph Adams. "The Influence of the French School on American Architecture." *American Architect,* L XVI (November 25, 1899).

Csikszentmihalyi, Mihaly. "Why We Need Things," from Steven Lubar and W. David Kingery, eds, *History From Things: Essays on Material Culture* (Washington D. C.: Smithsonian Institution Press, 1993).

Darton, Eric. *Divided We Stand: A Biography of New York City's World Trade Center*. New York: Basic Books, 2001.

de Botton, Alain. *The Architecture of Happiness*. New York: Vintage International, 2006.

DeFilippis, James. "From a Public Re-Creation to Private Recreation: The Transformation of Public Space in South Street Seaport." *Journal of Urban Affairs,* Vol 19, No. 4 (1997).

De Pol, John. "South Street." Woodcut, 1950.

Doratli, Naciye. "Revitalizing Historic Urban Quarters: A Model for Determining the Most Relevant Strategic Approach." *European Planning Studies,* Vol. 13, No. 5
(July 2005).

Downtown-Lower Manhattan Association, *Lower Manhattan Recommended Land Use.* 1st Report. DLMA First Report. S 2.3, B197, F1807. Record Group IV 3B 24; Box 197. DLMA Series 2.

Downtown-Lower Manhattan Association, Major Improvements Land Use Transportation Traffic. 2nd Report. November, 1963. DLMA 2nd Report, S2.4, B198, F1810. Record Group IV 3B 24, Box 198, DLMA Series 2.4 Bulletins & Publications.

Du Bois, W.E.B. *The Souls of Black Folk.* Rockville, MD: Arc Manor Publishers, 2008.

Ellul, Jacques. *The Technological Society.* New York: Alfred A. Knopf, 1985.

Esperdy, Gabrielle. "Ugly America; From the pages of Life, a complex view of the mid-century commercial landscape," *Places Journal* (Nov. 2014) https://placesjournal.org/article/ugly-america.

Farber, David, ed. *The Sixties; From Memory to History.* Chapel Hill: University of North Carolina Press, 1994. Kindle edition.

Fielder, Leslie. *The Art of the Essay.* New York: Crowell Publishers, 1958.

Filene, Benjamin. *Romancing the Folk: Public Memory and American Roots Music.* Chapel Hill: The University of North Carolina Press, 2000.

Fisher, James T. *On the Irish Waterfront; The Crusader, the Movie, and the Soul of the Port of New York*. Ithaca: Cornell University Press, 2009.

Fraunces Tavern. "Fraunces Tavern Museum Fact Sheet." NYHS, Guide to the Margot Gayle Papers 1959-2005, MS 241; Box 6, Folder 24: Fraunces Tavern.

Gallagher, Robert S. "South Street Seaport." *American Heritage Magazine*, October 1969.

Gayle, Margot. "Changing Scene: New York Then and Now." *Sunday News Magazine*, Oct. 16, 1983. N-YHS, Guide to the Margot Gayle Papers 1959-2005, MS 241; Box 6, Folder 24: Fraunces Tavern.

Gebhard, David. "The American Colonial Revival in the 1930s." *Winterthur Portfolio*, Vol 22, No. 2/3 (Summer-Autumn, 1987).

Gitlin, Todd. *The Sixties: Years of Hope, Days of Rage*. New York: Bantam Books, 1987.

Gleason, Gene. "South Street Ain't What She Used To Be...Yet." The *New York Times,* July 16, 1972.

Goodman, Paul. *Growing Up Absurd*. New York: Vintage Books, 1959.

Greatroix, Eliza. *Old New York from the Battery to Bloomingdale*. New York: 1875.

Guinness, Os. *The American Hour; A Time of Reckoning and the Once and Future Role of Faith*. New York: The Free Press, 1993.

Gurko, Leo. "The Heroic Impulse in *The Old Man and the Sea*." *The English Journal,* Vol. 44, No. 7 (Oct, 1955).

Guthrie, Arlo. "Alice's Restaurant," 1967.

Guthrie, Nora and The Woody Guthrie Archives. *My Name is New York: Ramblin' Around Woody Guthrie's Town.* Brooklyn: Powerhouse Books, 2012.

Hall, Peter. *Cities of Tomorrow.* Malden, MA: Blackwell Publishing, 2002.

Harper's Magazine

Decter, Midge. "Anti Americanism in America." Apr. 1968.

Goldman, Eric. "Good-by to the 'fifties - and good riddance," Jan. 1960.

Hutcheson, John C. "The Markets of New York." Jul. 1867.

Mailer, Norman. "On the Steps of the Pentagon." Mar. 1968.

Mailer, Norman. "Miami and Chicago." Nov. 1968.

Schlesinger, Arthur M. Jr. "America 1968: The Politics of Violence." Aug. 1968.

Vorse, Mary Heaton. "The Pirates' Nest of New York." Apr. 1952.

White, Charles Henry. "The Fulton Street Market." Sep. 1905.

White, Charles Henry. "In the Street." Feb. 1905.

Havens, Richie. *They Can't Hide Us Anymore.* New York: Avon, 1999.

Hayden, Dolores. *The Power of Place; Urban Landscapes as Public History.* Cambridge: MIT Press, 1995.

Heineman, Kenneth J. *Campus Wars; The Peace Movement at American State Universities in the Vietnam Era*. New York: New York University Press, 1994.

Hemingway, Ernest. *The Old Man and the* Sea. New York: Charles Scribner's Sons, 1952.

Huxtable, Ada Louise. *Goodbye History, Hello Hamburger; An Anthology of Architectural Delights and Disasters*. Washington D.C.: The Preservation Press, 1986.

Huxtable, Ada Louise. *The Unreal America: Architecture and Illusion*. New York: The New Press, 1997.

Isenberg, Alison. *Downtown America: A history of the place and the people who made it*. Chicago: University of Chicago Press, 2004.

Isserman, Maurice and Kazin, Michael. *America Divided: The Civil War of the 1960s* New York: Oxford University Press, 2008.

Jacobs, James B. *Mobsters, Unions, and Feds: The Mafia and the American Labor Movement*. New York: New York University Press, 2006.

Jacobs, James B., Coleen Friel, Robert Riddick. *Gotham Unbound: How New York City Was Liberated from the Grip of Organized Crime*. New York: New York University Press, 1999.

Jacobs, Jane. *The Death and Life of Great American Cities*. New York: Vintage Books, 1992.

Johnson, Malcolm. *On the Waterfront: The Pulitzer-Prize Winning Articles that Inspired the Classic Film and Transformed the New York Harbor*. New York: Chamberlain Bros., 2005.

Kaiser, Charles. *1968 In America; Music, Politics, Chaos, Counterculture, and the Shaping of a Generation.* New York: Grover Press, 1997.

Kammen, Michael. *Mystic Chords of Memory; the Transformation of Tradition in American Culture.* New York: Vintage Books, 1993.

Katz, Peter. *The New Urbanism; Towards an Architecture of Community.* New York: McGraw-Hill Inc., 1994.

Kasinitz, Philip, ed. *Metropolis; Center and Symbol of Our Times.* New York: New York University Press, 1995.

Kelly, Robert J. "The Last Waterfront: The Fulton Fish Market and the ILA as Family Businesses." In *The Upperworld and the Underworld; Criminal Justice and Public Safety.* New York: Kluwer Academic/Plenum Publishers, 1999.

Kurlansky, Mark. *1968: The Year that Rocked the World.* New York: Random House Trade Paperback, 2005.

Kurlalnsky, Mark. *The Big Oyster; History on the Half Shell.* New York: Ballantine Books, 2006.

Kulik, Gary. "America as Second Creation: Technology and Narrative of New Beginnings" *The Journal of Interdisciplinary History,* Vol 35, No 2 (Autumn 2004).

Landmarks Preservation Commission. *South Street Seaport Historic District Designation Report.* City of New York: 1977.

Lears, Jackson. *No Place of Grace; Antimodernism and the Transformation of American Culture, 1880-1920.* Chicago: University of Chicago Press, 1994.

Lehan, Richard. *The City in Literature: an Intellectual and Cultural History.* Berkeley, University of California Press, 1998.

Le Corbusier, Charles Edouard. *The Radiant City.* New York: Orion Press, 1967.

Lewis, Barry and Virginia Dajani. "The South Street Seaport Museum." *The Livable City; a publication of The Municipal Art Society* Vol 8 No.1 (June 1981).

LIFE Magazine. Internet archives. www.googlebooks.com.

Lindgren, James M. *Preserving South Street Seaport; The Dream and Reality of a New York Urban Renewal District.* New York: New York University Press, 2014.

Llosa, Mario Vargas & Thilo Ullman, "Hemingway," *Salmagundi,* No 128/129 (Fall 2000-Winter 2001).

Lowenthal, David. "Age and Artifact." In *Interpretation of Ordinary Landscapes,* ed. Douglas William Meinig. New York: Oxford University Press, 1979.

Lowenthal, David. *The Heritage Crusade and the Spoils of History.* Cambridge: Cambridge University Press, 1998.

Lubar, Steven and W. David Kingery, eds. *History from Things; Essays on Material Culture.* Washington D.C.: Smithsonian Institution Press, 1993.

Lewis, Peirce. "Common Landscapes as Historic Documents."

Leone, Mark P. and Barbara J. Little. "Artifacts as Expressions of Society and Culture: Subversive Genealogy and the Value of History."

Prown, Jules David. "The Truth of Material Culture: History or Fiction?"

Mann, Horace B. "Style in the Country House," *American Architect,* CVII (May 12, 1915).

Marling, Karal Ann. *George Washington Slept Here: Colonial Revivals and American Culture, 1876-1986.* Cambridge: Harvard University Press, 1988.

Marx, Leo. *The Machine In the Garden: Technology and the Pastoral Ideal in America.* New York: Oxford University Press, 2000.

Mason, Randall. *The Once and Future New York; Historic Preservation and the Modern City.* Minneapolis: University of Minnesota Press, 2009.

May, Bridget A. "Progressivism and the Colonial Revival: The Modern Colonial House, 1900-1920." *Winterthur Portfolio,* Vol 26 No. 2/3 (Summer-Autumn, 1991).

McKay, Richard C. *South Street; A Maritime History of New York.* New York: G.P. Putnamn's Sons, 1934.

McNulty, William C. "Docks, Fulton Market." Drypoint, c. 1930. Collection of the N-YHS.

Meikle, Jeffrey L. "Leo Marx's The Machine in the Garden," *Technology and Culture,* Vol 44 No 1 (Jan, 2003).

Meinig, Douglas William. *Interpretation of Ordinary Landscapes.* New York: Oxford University Press, 1979.

Metzger, John T. "The failed promise of a festival marketplace: South Street Seaport in lower Manhattan." *Planning Perspectives* Vol. 16 (2001).

Mielatz, Charles F. "Coenties Slip." Etching, 1890-91. Possession of the author.

Miller, Henry. *The Air-Conditioned Nightmare*. New York: New Directions Books, 1945.

Mitchell, Joni. "Woodstock," 1969.

Mitchell, Joseph. *Up in the Old Hotel*. New York: First Vintage Books, 1938, 1993.

Mitchell, Joseph. *My Ears Are Bent*. New York: Pantheon Books, 1938, 2001.

Mitchell, Joseph. *The Bottom of the Harbor, rev. ed.* New York: Pantheon Books, 2008.

Mollenkopf, John H. ed. *Power, Culture and Place: Essays on New York City*. USA: Russell Sage Foundation Publications, 1988.

Mumford, Lewis. *The Culture of Cities*. New York: Harcourt, Brace and Company, Inc., 1938.

Mumford Lewis. *Technics and Civilization*. Chicago: University of Chicago Press, 1962.

Mumford, Lewis. "Technics and the Nature of Man," *Technology and Culture*, Vol.7, No. 3 (Summer 1966).

Mumford, Lewis. *The Myth and The Machine: Technics and Human Development*. New York: Harcourt Brace Jovanovich, Inc., 1967.

National Endowment for the Humanities. *Humanities*, Nov/Dec 2014.

N-YHS, Guide to the Papers of Harmon Hendricks Goldstone 1906-1979 (Bulk 1966-1979) MS 25; Box 4, Folder 2: Landmarks Preservation Commission Reports (Nov 1978).

N-YHS, Guide to the Papers of Harmon Hendricks Goldstone 1906-1979 (Bulk 1966-1979) MS 25; Box 9, Folder 4: Fraunces Tavern.

N-YHS, Guide to the Margot Gayle Papers 1959-2005, MS 241; Box 6, Folder 24: Fraunces Tavern.

New York Preservation Archive Project, interview with Whitney North Seymour Jr., by Anthony C. Wood. July 29, 2006. http://www.nypap.org/content/whitney-north-seymour-jr-oral-history-interview

The New Yorker. "Our Footloose Correspondents, All Around The Town," April 23, 1966.

Kazan, Elia. *On the Waterfront,* 1954.

Osman, Suleiman. *The Invention of Brownstone Brooklyn; Gentrification and the Search for Authenticity in Postwar New York.* Oxford: Oxford University Press, 2011.

Page, Max. *The Creative Destruction of Manhattan, 1900-1940.* Chicago: University of Chicago Press, 1999.

Page, Max and Timothy Mennell, eds. *Reconsidering Jane Jacobs.* Chicago: American Planning Association Planners Press, 2011.

Page, Max and Randall Mason, editors. *Giving Preservation a History; Histories of Historic Preservation in the United States.* New York and London: Routledge, 2004.

Prochnau, William. *Once Upon a Distant War: David Halberstam, Neil Sheehan, Peter Arnet — Young War Correspondents and Their Early Vietnam Battles.* New York: Crown Publishing, 1995.

ProQuest Historical Newspapers, The *New York Times* (1851 - 2007).

Quart, Leonard. "Woody Allen's New York," in *The Films of Woody Allen; Critical Essays*, Charles L.P. Silet, ed. Lanham, MD: Scarecrow Press, Inc., 2006.

Rath, Frederick L. Jr. and the New York State Historical Association. "The South Street Maritime Museum Proposal and The Preservation of Schermerhorn Row in New York City; a Feasibility Study for the New York State Council on the Arts." (March 10, 1966). Rockefeller Archive Center, Record Group IV 3B 24, Series 2 D-LMA, Sub-series 2.3.

Reitano, Joanne. *The Restless City: A Short History of New York from Colonial Times to the Present*. New York: Routledge, 2010.

Rhodes, William B. "Colonial Revival and American Nationalism." *Journal of the Society of Architectural Historians,* Vol 35 No. 4 (Dec, 1976).

Richards, Keith. *Life*. Brown, Little & Company, 2011.

Rockefeller, David. *Memoirs*. New York: Random House, 2003.

Rockefeller Archive Center, Record Group IV 3B 24, D-LMA Projects South Street Seaport 1966. S 2.3, Box 167, Folder 1594.

Rockefeller Archive Center, Record Group IV 3B 24, Series 2 D-LMA, Sub-series 2.3 Projects, South Street Seaport, 1969-1972. Box 167, folder 1595.

Rockefeller Archive Center, D-LMA, D-LMA Projects: Marine Museums 1959-70. Series 2.3 Box 127 Folder 1321.

Rockefeller Archive Center, Record Group DLMA, Series 2, Sub-series 2.3 Projects South Street Seaport 1966, Box 167 Folder 1594.

Rockefeller Archive Center, Record Group DLMA, Projects/Landmarks, Jan. 1966– Sept. 1966.

Rockefeller Archive Center, DLMA Series 2.3 Projects, Landmarks. Record Group IV 3B 24, Box 112, Folder 1207; Nov 1966-Dec 1967.

Rockefeller Archive Center, DLMA Projects, Fraunces Tavern 1963-1990.

Rockefeller Archive Center, DLMA Series 2.3 Projects, Landmarks, 1965-1981. Record Group IV 3B 24, Box 112, folder 1203; Mar- Sept 1965.

Rockefeller Archive Center, Record Group DLMA Projects: Landmarks, Nov. 1966-Dec. 1967.

Rodgers, Daniel T. *Age of Fracture*. Cambridge, MA: Belknap Press, 2012.

Rodgers, Daniel T. *Atlantic Crossings: Social Politics in a Progressive Age*. Cambridge, MA: Belknap Press, 1998.

Rosebrock, Ellen. *South Street; a photographic guide to New York City's Historic Seaport*. New York: Dover Publications, Inc., 1974.

Rosenthal, Bernard. "The Urban Garden: Nineteenth-Century American Views of the City." *Texas Studies in Literature and Language,* Vol. 20 No. 1 (Spring 1978).

Rushing, Wanda. *Memphis and the Paradox of Place; Globalization in the American South*. Chapel Hill: University North Carolina Press, 2009.

Ryden, Kent C. "Why Your World Looks the Way It Does and Why It Matters: Cultural Landscape as Visual Culture." *Visual Arts Research,* Vol 32, No 2 (63). Papers Presented at a Visual Culture Gathering November 5-7, 2004. The Ohio State University, Columbus, Ohio (2006).

Rybczynski, Witold. *Makeshift Metropolis; Ideas About Cities.* New York: Scribner, 2010.

Seigel, Max. "Manhattan Landing Denounced by Three Borough Presidents," The *New York Times,* June 23, 1972.

Self, Robert O. and Thomas J. Sugrue, "The Power of Place: Race, Political Economy, and Identity in the Postwar Metropolis," in *A Companion To Post-1945 America,* Jean-Christophe Agnew & Roy Rosenzweig, eds. Malden, MA: Blackwell Publishing, 2006.

Simon, Paul. "Mrs. Robinson," 1967.

Snyder, Robert W. & Rebecca Zurier. "Picturing the City," in *Metropolitan Lives; The Ashcan Artists and Their New York.* New York: W.W. Norton & Company, 1995.

Smith, Joe. *Off the Record: An Oral History of Popular Music.* New York: Warner, 1988.

Sokol, Jason. *There Goes My Everything; White Southerners in the Age of Civil Rights, 1945-1975.* New York: Vintage Books, 2006.

Sontag, Susan. "Thirty Years Later," *The Three Penny Review.* Summer 1996.

South Street Seaport Museum. *South Street Seaport: A plan for a vital new historic center in Lower Manhattan.* New York City: South Street Seaport Museum, 1969. Rockefeller Archive Center Record Group Series 2: DLMA, Inc. Series 2.5: Reports and Studies.

South Street Seaport Museum. "South Street Seaport Museum" informational pamphlet, 1967. N-YHS, F 128.65 .S7 C65 1967.

South Street Seaport Museum. *South Street around 1900; The ships and men of a vanishing way of life photographed by Thomas W. Kennedy.* New York: South Street Seaport Museum, 1970. N-YHS F128.65 S7S8.

South Street Seaport Museum. *Map of Lower Manhattan, 1835.* Drawn by D.H. Burr.

Stanford, Alfred. *The Pleasures of Sailing.* New York: Simon and Schuster, 1943.

Stanford, Peter. "The Street of Ships in New York City." *Boating Magazine* (June, 1966). RAC Record Group IV 3B 24, Series DLMA 2, Sub-series 2.3 Projects South Street Seaport, Box 167 Folder 1595.

Stanford, Peter. *A Walk through South Street in the Afternoon of Sail.* New York: South Street Seaport Museum, 1967. N-YHS.

Stanford, Peter. "One Man's View of the Emergence of New York's New Sea Museum." *Curator,* Vol. 13, Iss. 4 (Oct. 1970).

Stanford, Peter. "We Could Do No Less then Respond with Loyalty," *Sea History* (Summer 1981).

Stanford, Peter and Norma. *A Dream of Tall Ships; How New Yorkers came together to save the city's sailing-ship waterfront.* Peekskill: Sea History Press, 2013.

Steinberg, Ted. *Gotham Unbound; The Ecological History of Greater New York.* New York: Simon and Schuster, 2014.

Stone, Robert. "American Dreamers: Melville and Kerouac," *The New York Times.* Dec 7, 1997.

Talley, Rhea. "The Genesis of the Williamsburg Restoration." *National Geographic,* Apr. 1937.

Teaford, Jon. *The Rough Road to Renaissance; Urban Revitalization in America, 1940-1985.* Baltimore: John Hopkins University Press, 1990.

Teaford, Jon. *The Twentieth-Century American City.* Baltimore: John Hopkins University Press, 1993.

Teaford, Jon. *The Metropolitan Revolution; The Rise of Post-Urban America.* New York: Columbia University Press, 2006.

Thelen, David. "Memory and American History," *The Journal of American History,* Vol. 75 No. 4 (March 1989).

TIME Magazine. Internet archives. www.timemagazine.com.

Trachtenberg, Alan. *The Incorporation of America: Culture and Society in the Gilded Age.* New York: Hill and Wang, 1982.

U.S. News and World Report. "Can the Big Cities Ever Come Back?" Sept 4, 1967.

Van Doren, Carl. Chapter 3 "Romance of Adventure," in *The American Novel.* New York: MacMillan, 1921.

West, Nathanael. *Day of the Locust.* USA: Aeonian Press, 1939.

White, E.B. *Here is New York.* New York City: The Little Bookroom, 1949, 1999.

Whittenmore, Katharine and Ellen Rosenbush. *The Sixties: Recollections of the Decade from Harper's Magazine.* New York: Franklin Square Press, 2010.

Whisnant, David. *All That Is Native and Fine; The Politics of Culture in an American Region.* Chapel Hill: The University of North Carolina Press, 2008.

Wilentz, Sean. *Chants Democratic: New York City and the Rise of the American Working Class.* Oxford: Oxford University Press, 2004.

Willis, Carol ed. *The Lower Manhattan Plan: The 1966 Vision for Downtown New York.* New York: Princeton Architectural Press, 2002.

Wilson, Richard Guy. *Re-creating the American Past; Essays on the Colonial Revival.* Charlottsville: University of Virginia Press, 2006.

Wolfe, Tom. *The Electric Kool-Aid Acid Test.* New York: Bantam Books, 1968.

Zipp, Samuel. *Manhattan Projects: The Rise and Fall of Urban Renewal in Cold War New York.* New York: Oxford University Press, 2010.

Zukin, Sharon. *Naked City; The Death and Life of Authentic Urban Places.* New York: Oxford University Press, 2010.

Made in the USA
Middletown, DE
12 March 2016